THE DEBATE

ON THE RULE OF CAUSE PREVENTION AND ITS STRICT IMPLEMENTATION

T0014892

WOMEN'S EMANCIPATION DURING THE PROPHET'S LIFETIME

THE DEBATE ON THE RULE OF CAUSE PREVENTION AND ITS STRICT IMPLEMENTATION

Volume 6

Abd al-Halim Abu Shuqqah

Translated and Edited by
Adil Salahi

KUBE
PUBLISHING

The Debate On the Rule of Cause Prevention And its Strict Implementation, Volume 6

First published in England by
Kube Publishing Ltd
Markfield Conference Centre,
Ratby Lane, Markfield,
Leicestershire, LE67 9SY,
United Kingdom
Tel: +44 (0) 1530 249230
Email: info@ kubepublishing.com
Website: www.kubepublishing.com

WOMEN'S EMANCIPATION DURING THE PROPHET'S LIFETIME

Copyright © Adil Salahi 2023
All rights reserved.

The right of Abd al-Halim Abu Shuqqah to be identified as the author of this work has been asserted by him in accordance with the Copyright, Designs and Patents Act, 1988.

CIP data for this book is available from the British Library.

ISBN: 978-1-84774-199-8 *Paperback*
ISBN: 978-1-84774-200-1 *Ebook*

Translated and Edited by: Adil Salahi
Cover Design by: Nasir Cadir
Typeset by: nqaddoura@hotmail.com
Printed by: Imak Offset, Turkey

Contents

CHAPTER III: Later Generations Go Too Far in Cause Prevention

Transliteration Table

Consonants. Arabic

initial, unexpressed, medial and final: ء ʾ

ا	a	د	d	ض	ḍ	ك	k
ب	b	ذ	dh	ط	ṭ	ل	l
ت	t	ر	r	ظ	ẓ	م	m
ث	th	ز	z	ع	ʿ	ن	n
ج	j	س	s	غ	gh	هـ	h
ح	ḥ	ش	sh	ف	f	و	w
خ	kh	ص	ṣ	ق	q	ي	y

Vowels, diphthongs, etc.

short:	ـَـ	a	ـِـ	i	ـُـ	u
long:	ـَـا	ā	ـُـو	ū	ـِـي	ī
diphthongs:			ـَـوْ	aw		
			ـَـىْ	ay		

CHAPTER I

A Balanced Islamic Approach to Cause Prevention

- Foreword
- The Divine Law's Balanced Approach
- Important Objectives for the Moderate Approach to Cause Prevention

Foreword

Some people argue that although a number of religious texts suggest that meeting between men and women is permissible, many scholars subscribe to the view that any such meeting should be disallowed under the rule of cause prevention. They say that by her very nature a woman is a source of temptation, and it is our duty to do what is needed to prevent such temptation.

We appreciate the motive of those who hold this view. They are saddened by the deterioration in the standards of morality. However, they, and others in the past, paint immorality as having gone way too far. Because of this exaggeration, they overlook the benefits of women's participation in the various life activities, and ignore the clear hardship, inconvenience and even moral corruption that results from disallowing such participation and meeting between the two sexes.

This argument of cause prevention is frequently advanced. In the process, it has led to overlooking and ignoring many religious texts. Therefore, we are devoting this volume to a discussion of the rule of cause prevention and its extreme implementation. Our discussion will show the effects of this hardline view on women as temptation.

The Divine Law's Balanced Approach

We will discuss the divine law's approach from two angles: (1) an explanation of some aspects of the divine law, and (2) an outline of how the law was implemented in the Prophet's lifetime.

Aspects of the divine law

The divine law establishes a clear balance between its objectives and its rules. Its objectives include that believers must address their worship most sincerely to God alone. They should learn what their faith requires of them. Moreover, they should keep their minds and hearts clear of all indecency, and they must cooperate in every good thing so as to build the best form of human life on earth. In order to achieve all these aims and objectives, Islam encourages women's participation in social life and permits meeting between men and women. At the same time, Islam confirms two of its rules: the prevention of what causes corruption and making things easy for believers. To explain, we may add:

One: Islam states that it is permissible for a woman to see men and for men to see women. It does not forbid this as a means of cause prevention. Instead, it establishes refined manners to prevent any temptation and allows men and women to see each other in a clean and pure atmosphere. God says: 'Tell believing men to lower their gaze and to be mindful of their chastity.' (24: 30) 'And tell believing women to lower their gaze and to be mindful of their chastity, and not to display their charms except what may ordinarily appear thereof. Let them draw their head-coverings over their bosoms.' (24: 31)

Two: At the same time, Islam permits women to meet with men, observing its clear manners. The Prophet said: 'Let no man be alone with one woman unless she is accompanied by a *maḥram*, (i.e a relative who is not permissible for her to marry).' (Related by al-Bukhari]

Three: Islam permits women to speak to men, establishing certain manners to ensure that this does not arouse temptation. God says: 'If you truly fear God, do not speak too softly, lest any who is sick at heart should be moved with desire; but speak in an appropriate manner.' (33: 32)

Four: Islam makes it clear that it is permissible for a woman to walk along roads and streets. It only requires her to refrain from what may excite temptation. God says: 'Do not display your charms as (women) used to display them in the old days of pagan ignorance.' (33: 33) 'Let them not swing their legs in walking so as to draw attention to their hidden charms.' (24: 31) Abu Mūsā al-Ashʿarī quotes the Prophet: 'Any woman who deliberately wears perfume and passes by some people so that they will smell her perfume is a fornicator.' (Related by al-Nasā'ī)

Five: Islam does not stop women from frequenting mosques in order to prevent the cause of temptation. On the contrary, it encourages women's attendance, provided that they observe the standards of decorum. Fāṭimah bint Qays reports: 'The announcement was made, 'All come to prayer', and I went ahead like many people. I was in the first row of women, which is the one immediately behind the last row of men.' (Related by Muslim) This announcement means that a prayer was about to be held and that it would be followed by a general meeting of the people. Fāṭimah's mention of her place shows that the rows of women are separated from those of men.

Abu Hurayrah said that God's Messenger (peace be upon him) said: 'The best of men's rows is the first and the best of women's rows is the last.' (Related by Muslim)

Zaynab, 'Abdullāh ibn Mas'ūd's wife, said: 'When any woman of you attends the mosque, she must not wear perfume.' (Related by Muslim)

Abu Hurayrah reports that God's Messenger (peace be upon him) said: 'Any woman who applies incense should not join us in 'Ishā Prayer.' (Related by Muslim)

Six: Islamic legislation reduces the *'awrah* of slave women, even though this increases temptation. Thus the *'awrah* of a slave woman is much less than that of a free woman.

This balanced approach to cause prevention is also used to ensure that women's participation in social life is safely conducted. Therefore, the Islamic approach overlooks some measure of temptation in order to make things easier for people. As slave women need to go out frequently on their masters' errands, they are allowed to uncover their heads and limbs. This is a practical example of how God, the Legislator, gives more importance to the rule of ease than the rule of cause prevention. We should note here that although slave women represent less temptation to free men because of their lower social status, nonetheless their temptation to slave men remains strong.[1]

- Anas reports: 'The Prophet (peace be upon him) stayed three days on the way between Khaybar and Madinah, to consummate his marriage to Ṣafiyyah bint Ḥuyay... Muslims said: "... If he screens her, she is a Mother of the Believers; but if he does not, she is his slave."' (Related by al-Bukhari and Muslim) This hadith shows that the Prophet's Companions were well aware of the distinction between the covering requirements for free and slave women. Their statement reflects that a distinction applied to the Prophet's women, whereby his wives were seen as distinct from his slave women.
- A report mentions that 'Umar saw a woman wearing a shawl and a head cover. On enquiring who she was, he was told that she was a slave. He said: 'A slave woman must not appear like her mistress.'
- A hadith related in al-Bukhari's *Ṣaḥīḥ* anthology mentions that a man stated some accusation against Sa'd ibn Abi Waqqāṣ. Sa'd supplicated: 'My Lord, if this servant of Yours is lying, extend his life, perpetuate his poverty and expose him to temptation.' 'Abd al-Malik ibn 'Umayr of the *tābi'īn* generation said: 'I saw him, with his eyebrows dropping over his eyes in old age. Yet he was harassing maids and staring at them as they passed by.' This hadith clearly shows that slave women were distinguished by their dress at the time of the

1. It should be noted that Islam abhorred slavery and enacted legislation for the freeing of slaves. However, as slavery was a world-wide system, it was not possible to abolish it altogether. Therefore, Islam stopped all sources of slavery except for war captives. Even these, its ultimate legislation was to either free them for a ransom or as an act of benevolence. What the author mentions about rules concerning slaves applied to the time when slavery was practised in all societies.

tābi'īn, which followed the Prophet's Companions' generation. This is indicated by the fact that the man was targeting slave women, who were less covered than free ones.

- Imam Mālik mentions that a slave woman may offer her prayers without covering her head. He said: "Such is her normal practice."
- Al-Mirghanānī, a distinguished Ḥanafī scholar, explains the reason for reducing slave women's *'awrah*, saying: 'Because a slave woman normally goes out on her master's errands wearing her household clothes.' Explaining this statement, another scholar, al-Kamāl ibn al-Hammām, said: 'The reason for giving the concession concerning the *'awrah* is the difficulty such a woman would have if the *'awrah* was extended to all her body, while she needs to go out frequently and attend to errands that require mixing with people.'

Features of implementation during the Prophet's lifetime

One: Clearly positive practices

We mention here some examples of practices during the Prophet's lifetime. We mentioned these, together with many more, in Volume 2 of this abridged series.

IN INDIVIDUAL CASES:

A woman riding behind a man. Asmā' bint Abu Bakr mentions that she was carrying a load on her head when the Prophet and a number of his Anṣārī Companions passed by her. 'The Prophet called me and then began to sit his camel so as to take me behind him.' This hadith is related by al-Bukhari and Muslim. It mentions that Asmā' did not take up the Prophet's offer to ride behind him on his camel, because she was aware of her husband's jealousy. In the commentary on this hadith in *Fatḥ al-Bārī*, al-Muhallab is quoted as saying that the hadith 'makes clear that it is permissible for a woman to ride behind a man, on the same mount, when they are moving with other riders.'[2]

This is a very significant case as it shows that the Prophet, who was with a number of his Companions, felt compassion towards Asmā' as she was carrying a heavy load on her head. He invited her to ride with him, and she most probably would have overcome her shyness and accepted the Prophet's offer, had she not felt that her husband's strong inclination towards jealousy did not allow her to do so.

Being with a friend's wife (but not in seclusion). Abu Juḥayfah narrated: 'The Prophet established a bond of brotherhood between Salmān and Abu al-Dardā.' Once Salmān went to visit Abu al-Dardā' and saw his wife wearing plain clothes. He asked her the reason and she told him: "Your brother, Abu al-Dardā', does not care for anything in this life."' (Related by al-Bukhari) This hadith mentions the case of a noble Companion of the Prophet entering the home of his brother in Islam when his wife was alone. He notices that she was wearing plain clothes and questions her about this. She tells him the reason without hesitation.

A woman proposes marriage to a devout man in the presence of other men. Sahl ibn Sa'd reports that "a woman came to the Prophet and said: 'Messenger of God! I have come to make of myself a present to you.' The Prophet looked up and down at her several times, then he lowered his head. When the woman realized that the Prophet did not make a decision concerning her offer, she sat down." (Related by al-Bukhari and Muslim)

2. While this is permissible when needed, the standards of propriety which we outlined in Volume 2 must be observed. One of these makes clear that there should be no physical contact between the man and the woman sharing the same mount. – Author's note.

Thābit al-Bunānī mentions that Anas said: 'A woman came to God's Messenger offering herself as a present to him. Anas's daughter said: "How deprived of shyness." Anas said: She is better than you. She wanted to marry the Prophet and she offered herself to him.' (Related by al-Bukhari)

Al-Bukhari relates this hadith under the chapter heading: 'A woman's offer of marriage to a devout man.' Ibn Ḥajar says in *Fatḥ al-Bārī*: 'A case of al-Bukhari's subtle observations is that he was aware of the special case that allows a woman to make of herself a gift to the Prophet, which means that she marries him without requesting a dowry. Yet he deduces from the hadith a general rule which allows a woman to offer herself in marriage to a devout man, because she admires his devotion.

We should note how Anas's daughter objected to this woman's attitude on two counts: her offering herself and doing so in public. Her father, Anas, who was educated by the Prophet himself and was experienced life in the society established by the Prophet, felt that there was nothing wrong on either count. He knew that women shared fully in the social life of the Muslim society during the Prophet's lifetime.

In public situations

In the mosque: Al-Rubayyiʿ bint Muʿawwidh ibn ʿAfrā' said: 'We used to fast on that day (i.e. 10 al-Muḥarram) after that, and we used to let our children fast as well. (Muslim adds here: and we would go to the mosque) We made woollen toys for them.' (Related by al-Bukhari and Muslim)

This is a situation when al-Rubayyiʿ and other Muslim women used to go to the mosque and keep their children occupied so that they could finish their fast. We need to remember here that Muslim women attended the Prophet's mosque for no less than twelve different purposes, namely, offering obligatory prayers including Friday Prayer, joining non-obligatory prayers such as funeral and eclipse prayers, *i'tikāf*, visiting a person during his *i'tikāf*, learning, spending spare time with other women, attending a public meeting, attending a celebration, attending the judgement of disputes, nursing the wounded, cleaning the mosque and sleeping in the mosque.

Celebrating the Eid. Umm 'Aṭiyyah narrated: 'We were ordered to go out on Eid Day, including virgin girls who were brought out of their seclusion. We even brought out those who were in menstruation. They stayed behind the congregation, glorifying God as the congregation did and supplicated as they did, eager to receive the blessings and benefit of that day.' (Related by al-Bukhari and Muslim)

We note how the Prophet insisted on all women attending the Eid Prayer, including young and virgin women who were normally not allowed to go out. They remained at home until they were married. Indeed, the Prophet ordered those who were menstruating and could not therefore pray to attend. They would witness and share the blessing of that day.

Joining the army. Ḥafṣah reported: 'A woman came... She mentioned her sister. She said that her sister's husband 'joined the Prophet on twelve military expeditions, with my sister accompanying him on six of these.' (Related by al-Bukhari) This hadith confirms that one woman joined her husband on six military expeditions led by God's Messenger (peace be upon him). This means that women did things that definitely involved mixing with men.

We, thus, note that God's Messenger (peace be upon him) approved all these aspects of women's participation in social life, despite the possibility of temptation. This makes clear that we should overlook such possibility as long as it does not become very common.

Two: The Prophet's firm measures of cause prevention

- Abu Sa'īd al-Khudrī quotes the Prophet (peace be upon him): 'Do not sit by the road side.' People said: 'We cannot do without that. These are our places where we sit and chat together.' He said: 'If you have to, then give the road its due rights.' They asked: 'What is the right of the road'? He said: 'Lowering one's gaze, removing harm, returning greeting, enjoining what is right and forbidding evil.' (Related by al-Bukhari and Muslim)

The hadith shows that the Prophet noticed that some unacceptable results are caused by people sitting together by the roadside, including causing women some embarrassment and exposing men to some temptation. In order to prevent the cause of these, he thought of taking a measure that prevented such consequences. He gave the order not to sit by the roadside. However, he then realized that this measure caused men some inconvenience. They expressed this saying: 'We cannot do without that. These are our places where we sit and chat together.' The Prophet, therefore, abandoned the original measure, replacing it by allowing what he wanted to prevent, but he outlined certain manners that they must observe when they sit together. These were meant to reduce what stirred temptation while maintaining friendly relations between believers, strengthening their social bonds. These were 'lowering one's gaze, removing harm, returning greeting, enjoining what is right and forbidding evil.'

- 'Abdullāh ibn 'Abbās narrated: 'On the Day of Sacrifice, the Prophet (peace be upon him) took al-Faḍl ibn 'Abbās behind him on the back of his she-camel. Al-Faḍl was a handsome man. The Prophet stopped to answer people's questions. A pretty woman from Khath'am came to the Prophet to ask him for a ruling. Al-Faḍl looked at her and admired her beauty. The Prophet turned back as al-Faḍl was looking at her. He put his hand back and held al-Faḍl's chin moving his face away from her.' (Related by al-Bukhari and Muslim)

The Prophet's action had two objectives. The first and immediate one, stated in the hadith, is to physically remove what is prohibited in Islam. The second objective is to deal with the temptation resulting from staring at a woman's face. This is achieved by ordering men to lower their gaze when they face a woman. It is not dealt with by commanding women to cover their faces. Lowering men's gaze is attained through education and instruction on the one hand and strengthening social responsibility, mutual advice, enjoining right and prohibiting evil on the other.

☙ Sahl ibn Sa'd reported: 'When they joined the Prophet in prayer, some people tied their lower garments around their necks because they were short. Therefore, the women were ordered not to lift their heads from prostration until the men had actually sat down.' (Related by al-Bukhari and Muslim)

God's Messenger (peace be upon him) noticed that some of his Companions wore short garments, due to their poverty. When they prostrated themselves, some of their *'awrah* might be exposed when they moved. Therefore, he ordered the women to observe this simple practice, so that the cause of temptation did not arise. He did not resort to the stringent measure of cause prevention, which would have disallowed women from going to the mosque.

☙ Umm Salamah reported: 'When God's Messenger finished the prayer with *salam*, the women would then leave. He stayed in his place for a short while.' Ibn Shihāb said: 'I think that he stayed on to allow the women to depart before any men could catch up with them, but God knows best.' (Related by al-Bukhari)

This is confirmed by the hadith in which the Prophet says: 'Perhaps we should leave this door for women.' It appears that the Prophet noticed that some men who left immediately when the prayer was finished caused jostling or crowding at the gates, with men and women leaving at the same time. This might be a cause of temptation for men and women alike. Therefore, he suggested this measure to prevent any such occurrence. He did not, however, stop women from going to the mosque as cause prevention.

- ʿAbdullāh ibn ʿAmr ibn al-ʿĀṣ narrated: 'God's Messenger (peace be upon him) stood on the platform and said: "After this day of mine, no man may enter the place of a woman whose husband is absent unless he is accompanied by one or two men."' (Related by Muslim)

It seems that the Prophet was informed of some problem arising from a man entering the place of a woman whose husband was away, for some legitimate reason. To prevent the occurrence of temptation, the Prophet ordered this precaution. He did not disallow men from entering the places of women in all cases.

- ʿĀ'ishah mentioned that the Prophet (peace be upon him) used to examine women who migrated to join him, as required by the verse that says: 'Believers! When believing women come to you as migrants, test them.' (60:10) When any migrant woman submitted to this test, the Prophet said to her verbally: 'I accept your pledge of allegiance.' 'By God, his hand never touched a woman's hand when she pledged allegiance.' (Related by al-Bukhari and Muslim)
- A hadith entered in *al-Muwaṭṭa'* and narrated by Umaymah bint Ruqayqah says: 'Women said to the Prophet: "We are ready to pledge allegiance to you, Messenger of God." He said: "I do not shake hands with women."'

At this point, the Prophet held back his hand and said: 'I do not shake hands with women.' This is a proper measure to prevent the occurrence of temptation. The reason is that the Prophet wanted to ensure that none of the women felt any temptation due to the shaking of hands. Thus, the pledge of allegiance to the ruler continues to be given by women, but is done so verbally, not by shaking hands. We note that when the Prophet was certain that in the cases of Umm Sulaym and Umm Ḥarām, no temptation was feared, he allowed them to touch him. This shows that a general rule of manners may carry some exception in certain scenarios of men being together with women, and when temptation is totally unlikely, either because of family relations or close friendship or some other consideration.

Three: Women continued to participate in social life despite some shortfalls

When we review the cases of women's participation in social life and their mixing with men during the Prophet's lifetime, which we mentioned in Volume 2 of this abridged version, we realize that many of them took place towards the end of the Prophet's life. This means that despite the occurrence of some unfortunate slippages, women's participation continued to be an essential feature of Islamic society. It also shows that the Prophet did not consider that such events required taking any further measures. He rather considered that the observation of Islamic manners was sufficient for the general prevention of temptation. Individual cases of violation are unfortunate, but they are part and parcel of human life, and no human society can be completely free of these, not even during the Prophet's lifetime. This despite the fact that the Prophet describes his own generation as the best of all generations. We will cite some examples of such errors, including those involving the greatest indecency, with the perpetrator expressing no repentance before the case was reported to the ruler.

- Ibn Mas'ūd narrated that 'A man kissed a woman....' In a different version: 'A man kissed or handled a woman....' Yet another version mentions that the man said: 'I flirted with a woman in the far end of Madinah but did not have intercourse with her.' He came to the Prophet (peace be upon him) and told him. God revealed the verse that says: "Attend to your prayers at both ends of the day and in the early watches of the night. Surely, good deeds erase evil ones." (11: 114) The man said: 'Messenger of God, does this apply to me?' He said: 'It applies to all my community.' (Related by al-Bukhari and Muslim)

- Anas narrated: 'A man came to the Prophet and said: "Messenger of God, I have committed a punishable offence. Enforce it on me." The prayer was then called and he joined the congregational prayer led by God's Messenger (peace be upon him). When the prayer was over, the man again said: "Messenger of God, I have committed a punishable offence. Enforce it on me." The Prophet said: "Did you offer the prayer with us?" The man said: "Yes." The Prophet said: "You have been forgiven."' (Related by Muslim)
- Jābir ibn Samurah narrated: 'God's Messenger was brought a short muscular man with thick hair, wearing a lower garment. He had committed adultery. The Prophet turned him away twice, but then he ordered the enforcement of mandatory punishment. The man was then stoned. The Prophet said: "Will it be that whenever we set out to fight for God's cause that someone from among you strongly feels the sexual urge and commits adultery? If God hands any such person to me, I shall severely punish him."'
- 'Abdullāh ibn Buraydah narrated from his father: 'The Ghāmidī woman came to the Prophet and said: "Messenger of God, I have committed adultery. Purify me." The Prophet told her to go home. The following day, she said to him: "Messenger of God, why do you send me back? Perhaps you are sending me back as you did with Mā'iz! By God, I am pregnant...." (After she had weaned the child, she came to) the Prophet and he gave the child to a Muslim man. He then

gave instructions and a hole was dug for her up to her chest. He told people to stone her.' (Related by Muslim)

- 'Imrān ibn Ḥuṣayn reported that a woman from the Juhaynah tribe came to the Prophet and she was pregnant through adultery. She said: 'Prophet, I have committed an offence with a mandatory punishment. Enforce it on me.' The Prophet called in her guardian. He said to him: 'Treat her kindly. When she has given birth, bring her to me.' The guardian did that. The Prophet gave instructions. Her garments were tied up on her. He then gave orders. She was stoned and he offered the funeral prayer for her....' (Related by Muslim)
- Wā'il al-Kindī reported that 'A woman was raped by a man as she was going to the mosque in the darkness at dawn. She appealed to a passer-by for help, but the rapist ran away. Then a group of people passed by her and she appealed to them for help. They caught up with the one to whom she had appealed but the other (i.e. the rapist) managed to run away. They brought her the man they caught. He said to her: 'I am the one who helped you, but the other has run away. They took him to God's Messenger (peace be upon him)....' (Related by Ahmad)
- Abu Hurayrah and Zayd ibn Khālid al-Juhanī narrated: "A man came to the Prophet and said to him: 'I appeal to you by God to judge between us according to God's Book.' His opponent, who was more learned, stood up and said: 'He makes a fair request. Please judge between us according to God's Book, but let me speak first.' The Prophet told him to say what he wanted. He said: 'My son was working for this man and he committed adultery with his wife. I settled the case with him by giving him 100 sheep and a servant. I then asked some learned people and they told me that my son's punishment is 100 lashes and that he be sent into exile for a year, while this man's wife is to be stoned.' The Prophet

said: 'By Him who holds my soul in His hand, I will judge between you two according to God's Book: the sheep and the servant are to be returned to you. Your son is to be whipped 100 lashes and sent into exile for a year. You, Unays, go to this man's wife and ask her. If she confesses her guilt, then stone her.' She admitted her guilt and she was stoned." (Related by al-Bukhari and Muslim)

- Ibn ʿAbbās reported that Hilāl ibn Umayyah accused his wife of having committed adultery. He came forward and testified, (meaning that he called God four times to witness that he was indeed telling the truth; and the fifth time, that God's curse be upon him if he was telling a lie). The Prophet said to them that God knew that one of them was lying; but would either of them turn to God in repentance? His wife stood up and testified, (meaning that she called God four times to witness that he was indeed telling a lie; and the fifth time, that God's wrath be upon her if he was telling the truth). (Related by al-Bukhari and Muslim)
- Sahl ibn Saʿd al-Sāʿidī narrated: '... ʿUmayr came in until he reached God's Messenger among the people. He said: "Messenger of God, if a man finds another man with his own wife and he kills him: would you kill him (in retaliation]? Or, what should he do?" God's Messenger said: "God has given revelation about your case with your wife. Go and bring her." Sahl said: They exchanged oaths and curses. I was among the people attending God's Messenger (peace be upon him).'
- Abu Hurayrah and Zayd ibn Khālid narrated: 'God's Messenger (peace be upon him) was asked about a slave woman who is unmarried and commits fornication. He said: "If she commits unlawful sexual intercourse punish her by flogging; then if she commits it again, flog her; then if again, flog her then sell her even for a paltry price.' (Related by al-Bukhari and Muslim)

- Abu ʿAbd al-Raḥmān narrated that ʿAlī delivered a speech and said: ʻPeople, enforce the mandatory punishment (for adultery) on your slaves, whether they are married or unmarried. A maid belonging to God's Messenger committed adultery, and he commanded me to flog her. I found out that she had recently given birth. I (refrained], fearing that if I flog her, I might kill her. I mentioned this to the Prophet and he said: ʻYou have done well.' (Related by Muslim)
- ʿAbdullāh ibn ʿUmar narrated: ʻThe Jews came to the Prophet and said that a man and a woman from among them committed adultery. The Prophet asked them: "What does the Torah say about stoning?" They said: "We shame them and flog them." ʿAbdullāh ibn Sallām said: "You lie. The Torah includes a verse mentioning stoning. They brought the Torah and opened it. One of them covered the stoning verse with his hand and recited the verses before and after it. ʿAbdullāh ibn Sallām told him to remove his hand. When he did, the stoning verse was clearly seen. They said: "Muhammad, he has told the truth. It mentions the stoning verse." God's Messenger gave orders and both were stoned. I saw the man bending over the woman to protect her from the stones.' (Related by al-Bukhari and Muslim)

From all these cases we can conclude that the Prophet's teaching does not resort to measures that are too stringent. We do not see any extreme fear from temptation. The Prophet does not take special measures as a result of a few individual cases that inevitably occur in all human societies. What is needed when such situations occur is to highlight their unacceptability and their serious effect on society. In other words, education and guidance are enough to counter them, in addition to the enforcement of deterrent punishments on the offenders. It is wrong to try to enact more stringent legislation that causes much inconvenience to people.

Four: The Prophet disapproves of strictness generally, but particularly in relation to women perceived as temptation

God, the Wise Legislator, has mapped out the way to protect society from temptation. Had He known that the established standards were inadequate, He would have enacted more in order to protect Muslims and their honour. God's Messenger (peace be upon him) said to his Companions: 'Do you wonder at Saʿd's protective jealousy? I am even more protective than him, and God is more protective than me.' He also said: 'None is more protective than God. Therefore, He has forbidden all indecency.' (Both hadiths are related by al-Bukhari and Muslim) However, extreme strictness in religious matters goes far back in history. One aspect of it is stated by Anas: 'When a Jewish woman was in menstruation, her people would not allow her to join them for their meals or drinks or to stay with them in their homes. The Prophet's Companions asked him about this, and God revealed the verse that says: "They ask you about menstruation. Say: it is an unclean condition...."' (2: 222) God's Messenger told them that they may join women for their meals, drinks and at home. Essentially, they were permitted to do everything with them except have sexual intercourse. Another aspect of extreme strictness is reported by Abu Mūsā: 'It was the practice of the Children of Israel that if urine fell on a person's skin, he would scrub it off with a sharp instrument.' (Related by al-Bukhari and Muslim)

God's Messenger has warned us against following in the footsteps of earlier communities that deviated from divine guidance. Extreme strictness is one aspect of such deviation. Abu Saʿīd al-Khudrī mentions that the Prophet said: 'You shall follow the methods of earlier communities, one span after another and one cubit after another. Were they to go into a lizard's hole, you shall follow them into it.' We said: 'Are you referring to the Jews and Christians?' He said: 'Who else?' (Related by al-Bukhari)

In His infinite mercy, God has given us, Muslims, an easy code of law that warns us against all types of extremism. God's Messenger tells the truth: 'This religion is easy. Whoever pulls hard against this religion shall be defeated.' (Related by al-Bukhari) The Prophet also says: 'Ruined are the pedantic! Ruined are the pedantic! Ruined are the pedantic!' (Related by Muslim) He also says: 'Beware against extremism in religion. Communities before you were ruined by being extremist in religion.' (Related by al-Nasā'ī)

The Prophet took very firm measures when any aspect of extremism appeared in his community. Anas ibn Mālik reports: 'Three people came to the Prophet's home enquiring about his worship. When they were told its details, they seemed to think it too little and thought: How can we compare ourselves to the Prophet when God has forgiven him his past and future sins? One of them said: "As for me, I shall pray the whole night, every night." Another said: "As for me, I shall fast every day and never spend a day without fasting." The third said: "And as for me, I shall stay away from women and will never marry." God's Messenger went to them and said: "Are you the ones who said so-and-so? I am the one among you all who fears God most, but I fast some days and do not fast on others; I pray and sleep at night; and I marry women. Whoever dislikes my practice does not belong to me."' (Related by al-Bukhari and Muslim)

Another scenario is reported by 'Ā'ishah: 'The Prophet did something, showing that it is a concession, but some people steered away from it (feeling it lenient]. The Prophet (peace be upon him) was informed and he addressed the people. (In Muslim's version: anger was visible on his face) He praised God, then said: "How come that some people steer away from something that I do? By God, I am the one who knows God best and the one who fears Him most."' (Related by al-Bukhari and Muslim)

‘Umar ibn Abu Salamah, the Prophet’s stepson, reports that he asked God’s Messenger (peace be upon him): ‘May a fasting person kiss (his wife]?’ The Prophet said: ‘Ask this one’, pointing to Umm Salamah. She told him that God’s Messenger did so. He said: ‘Messenger of God, God has forgiven you your past and future sins.’ The Prophet said to him: ‘By God, I am the one among you who fears God most.’ (Related by Muslim)

‘Ā’ishah reports that a man came to the Prophet seeking a ruling. She was listening behind the door. He said: ‘Messenger of God, the time of Fajr Prayer becomes due when I am in a state of ceremonial impurity. May I fast?’ God’s Messenger said: ‘I, too, may be in a state of ceremonial impurity when the Fajr Prayer becomes due, and I do fast on that day.’ The man said: ‘Messenger of God, you are unlike us, as God has forgiven you your earlier and later sins.’ The Prophet said: ‘By God, I hope that I am the most God-fearing among you and the one who knows best what to avoid.’ (Related by Muslim)

The Prophet’s Companions followed his guidance, disapproving whatever he disapproved of. There are numerous such relevant examples, but here are just a few:

- Zurārah mentions that Sa‘d ibn Hishām ibn ‘Āmir wanted to join a jihad campaign. ‘He came to Madinah intending to sell a real estate property he owned and use the price to buy arms and horses. He intended to fight against the Byzantines until he died. When he arrived in Madinah, he met some people there. They advised him against doing this. They told him that six people wanted to do the same during the Prophet’s lifetime, but the Prophet ordered them not to do so. He said to them: “Will you not follow my example?” When they mentioned this to Sa‘d ibn Hishām, he reinstated his marriage with his wife whom he had divorced earlier. He asked people to witness the reinstatement of his marriage....’ (Related by Muslim)

- Abu Wā'il reports: 'Abu Mūsā was too strict about urination... Ḥudhayfah said: 'I wish he would stop. God's Messenger (peace be upon him) stopped by the rubbish heap of certain people and urinated standing.' (Related by al-Bukhari)
- Muhammad ibn Sīrīn reports that ''Umar ibn al-Khaṭṭāb was with a group of people and they were reciting the Qur'an. 'Umar then went away to relieve himself. He continued to recite the Qur'an on his way back. Someone said to him: "Are you reciting the Qur'an when you have not performed a new ablution?" 'Umar said to him: "Who has given you this ruling? Was it Musaylamah?"[3] (Related by Mālik)
- Muhammad ibn al-Muntashir said that he mentioned to 'Ā'ishah that Ibn 'Umar said: 'I do not like to be smelling of perfume when I enter into consecration.' She said: 'May God grant mercy to Abu 'Abd al-Raḥmān. I used to apply perfume to God's Messenger (peace be upon him), and he would visit his wives, then start his consecration in the morning, carrying a strong perfume scent.' (Related by al-Bukhari and Muslim)
- 'Ubaydullāh ibn 'Abdullāh ibn 'Umar mentions that a slave woman belonging to his father committed adultery. Ibn 'Umar beat her on her feet and back. I quoted the verse (referring to adulterers]: 'Let no compassion for them keep you from carrying out this law of God.' (24: 2) He said: 'Son, did you see me treat her with compassion? God has not ordered me to kill her or flog her on her head. I have beaten her up, giving her pain.'
- 'Abd al-Raḥmān ibn Yazīd al-Anṣārī reports: 'Anas ibn Mālik returned from Iraq. Abu Ṭalḥah (his stepfather) and Ubay ibn Ka'b visited him. He served them cooked food and they

---

3. Musaylamah was one who alleged that he was a prophet. He earned the title, 'the liar', for his false claim. 'Umar's response indicates that there was no basis for the view expressed by his interlocutor.

ate. Then Anas performed a fresh ablution. Both Abu Ṭalḥah and Ubay ibn Ka'b said: "What is this, Anas? Following the Iraqi practice"? Anas said: "I wish I had not done that." Abu Ṭalḥah and Ubay ibn Ka'b stood up and prayed without performing a fresh ablution.'[4]

- Zayd ibn Thābit's daughter was informed that some women asked for light in the middle of the night to ascertain whether they had finished their periods. She criticized their practice and said: 'Women used not to do that.'[5] (Related by Mālik)

All these situations clearly disapprove of taking a hard line that is contrary to facilitating the implementation of the divine law and making it easy for people. Such a hard line either disallows what Islam permits, or abandons it as unworthy, or imposes what Islam does not make obligatory. We will now cite some examples of how the Prophet, his Companions and their successors disapproved of adopting a hard line regarding the temptation presented by women in particular.

- Sa'd ibn Abi Waqqāṣ said: 'The Prophet refused 'Uthmān's ibn Maẓ'ūn's suggestion. Had he agreed to his request of celibacy, we would have emasculated ourselves.' A different version related by al-Ṭabarānī is as follows: ''Uthmān ibn Maẓ'ūn said: "Messenger of God, I find celibacy too hard. Permit me to emasculate myself." The Prophet said: "No. Resort to fasting instead."'
- 'Abdullāh ibn Mas'ūd reported: 'We used to go on jihad with God's Messenger (peace be upon him), and we had nothing.

4. The point here is that eating cooked food does not require a fresh ablution, if one's initial ablution is still valid. Their question implied disapproval of following an Iraqi practice in preference to the practice of the people of Madinah who learnt it directly from the Prophet.
5. This is a situation of taking the trouble to wake up in the middle of the night in order to establish cleanliness from menstruation. There is no need for this. Waiting until the morning is perfectly permissible.

(In Muslim's version: we had no women) We thought of emasculating ourselves, but God's Messenger forbade us.' (Related by al-Bukhari and Muslim)

- Abu Hurayrah reports that he said: 'Messenger of God, I am a young man and I fear that I find things hard. I cannot afford to get married. The Prophet gave me no answer. I later said the same and he gave me no answer. I again said the same and he gave me no answer. I said it once more, and the Prophet said to me: "Abu Hurayrah, whatever you shall have has been written and the ink has dried, and it will be the same whether you emasculate yourself or not."' (Related by al-Bukhari)
- 'Ā'ishah said: 'Messenger of God, shall all people return having earned two rewards and I go back having one reward?' He instructed 'Abd al-Raḥmān ibn Abu Bakr to take me to al-Tan'īm. 'He took me behind him on his camel. I would drop my headcover, uncovering my neck. He hit my leg pretending to hit his mount. I said to him: Do you see anyone around?' (Related by Muslim)
- 'Abdullāh ibn 'Umar mentioned that God's Messenger said: 'Do not prevent women from coming to the mosque at night.' One of 'Abdullāh's sons said: 'We will not let them come out, lest they use it for pretence.' Ibn 'Umar rebuked him. (In another version: he hurled such abuse on him as I had never heard him say) He said: 'I say that God's Messenger said such-and-such, and you say that you shall prevent them'! (Related by Muslim)

Imam Ibn Ḥajar said: 'It appears that his son said this because he noticed that some women took a casual attitude, and he felt very protective. 'Abdullāh's hard stance towards his son is cited as the right way to discipline a person who objects to the Sunnah on the basis of his own opinion, or objects to a scholar by sheer personal preference.'

- Ibn Jurayj said: 'Aṭā' reported to me from Jābir ibn 'Abdullāh: 'The Prophet started on the day of Eid al-Fiṭr by offering the Eid Prayer. He then delivered his sermon. When he finished, he came down and went up to the women to admonish them...' I said to 'Aṭā': Do you consider that it is a duty of the imam to remind the women?' He said: 'It is indeed their duty, but why do they not do it'? (Related by al-Bukhari and Muslim)

Imam Ibn Ḥajar said that *Qadi* 'Iyāḍ claimed that the Prophet's admonition of the women occurred during his speech after the prayer, which means that he did not address any admonition specially for women. He added that this was in the early period of Islam, which means that it was before the *ḥijāb* was ordered. He further said that it applied to the Prophet alone because he was immune to temptation. Imam al-Nawawī expressed disagreement, citing this hadith which clearly states that the Prophet's admonition addressed to the women was after he had finished his *khuṭbah*, as the hadith says: 'When it (i.e. the sermon) was finished, he went up to the women.' Special concessions given to the Prophet cannot be taken on the basis of probability. That 'Aṭā' says: 'It is indeed their duty' shows that 'Aṭā' was of this view.

- Ḥafṣah bint Sīrīn said: 'We used to prohibit our adolescent women from going out to prayer on the Eid occasions. A woman came to our place and resided in the palace of Bani Khalaf. She reported as regards her sister: "My sister asked the Prophet whether a woman who had no top garment need not attend the Eid Prayer." He said: "Let her sister give her of her own garments, so that she will attend the goodness there and take part in the Muslims' supplication." When Umm 'Aṭiyyah arrived I asked her: "Did you hear that from the Prophet"? She said: "Yes, may my father be sacrificed for him – it was her practice to say this whenever she mentioned the Prophet – I heard him saying: "All young women and those who normally stay indoors and the ones having their periods should come, to attend the goodness and take part in the believers' supplication. Those menstruating, however, should remain outside the praying area."'"'

Ibn Ḥajar comments: 'It appears that they used to stop adolescent women from going out because they felt the standard of morality deteriorated after the first Islamic generation, but the Prophet's Companions did not approve of this. They felt that the ruling remained the same as it was during the Prophet's lifetime.

☙ Ibn Jurayj said: 'We mentioned to 'Aṭā' that Ibn Hishām did not allow women to perform the *ṭawāf* alongside women.' He said: "How can he disallow them when the Prophet's wives performed the *ṭawāf* alongside men"'? (Related by al-Bukhari)

Ibn Ḥajar said that Ibn Hishām did not allow women to perform the *ṭawāf* at any time when the men were performing it. Hence, 'Aṭā''s censure, based on what 'Ā'ishah did.

Five: The Prophet shows the way to deal with life's temptations

Temptation is best overcome when properly confronted

To confront the different types of temptation that a person may face in life is the best way to overcome them. This is most clearly explained by God's Messenger (peace be upon him). The fact is that life's temptations never end. For any person, they only come to an end when they die. As for mankind generally, they only stop when the Last Hour arrives. Moreover, they are present everywhere, even in a place of worship or a hermitage. They may occur in any environment, even that of worship or teaching and learning. In such places of purity and such fine activities, a believer may yield to the temptation of achieving high status and reputation. Therefore, it is not possible to evade and resist temptation through running away from what is permissible, or prohibiting what God has made permissible, or by imposing barriers that God does not sanction.

What is necessary is to lead a life that opens all legitimate fields and aspects, while all the time resisting whatever temptation it throws at us. A Muslim's life is full of different ways of facing and resisting temptation. Therefore, a mixed way of life where men and women meet, and they all resist temptation, is the natural and healthy approach. This is the one the Prophet taught to his Companions. He organized all affairs of society on this basis, including women's participation in social life. He opened the way for a Muslim woman to migrate when she is exposed to religious persecution. He admitted her into the mosque, without separation between men and women, whether during prayer and worship or when attending a public meeting. It is perfectly permissible for a woman to attend and nurse the wounded, participate in a legitimate activity in her spare time, attend celebrations, etc. It is also appropriate for women to perform the duties of pilgrimage and attend the Eid prayers alongside men. Women may also enjoin what is right, censure what is wrong and forbidden, request and offer favours in the same way as men and with them. Needless to say, women may also give their pledge of allegiance to Muslim rulers. We cited many examples of women's participation in all these and similar activities in Volume 2 of this series.

It is a Muslim's religious duty to persevere in resisting temptation, however hard it may be. This is what the Prophet taught his Companions and encouraged them to practise. When some of them found it hard and contemplated evasion, the Prophet disapproved and required that they remain steadfast in resisting temptation. One such example is that mentioned earlier of the Prophet's disapproval of their suggestion to emasculate themselves when they had no legitimate way to fulfil their sexual desire.

Every Muslim, man or woman, is bound to gain much through resisting temptation. It makes them better able to face the general difficulties of life, and ready to encounter and overcome even harder temptations. It gives them a better understanding of the nature of life. This helps a Muslim to develop a better balanced personality. Moreover, a Muslim may earn double reward: one for dealing with and resisting temptation and one for setting a proper objective for women's participation in social life.

The role of a Muslim's refined conscience in resisting temptation

As mentioned earlier, the best way to deal with temptation is to confront and resist it. The Prophet made this clear and he laid down the most important basis for successful resistance. This is achieved through nurturing and refining the conscience of Muslim men and women. Generally speaking, the Qur'an educates and guides a Muslim's conscience as it is the primary factor in all the activities of every Muslim, including the time when men and women meet. The Prophet's Sunnah consolidates this education and provides details of what the Qur'an mentions in general. Let us reflect on this outline of the Islamic character as given in the Qur'an:

> Truly, successful shall be the believers, who humble themselves in their prayer, who turn away from all that is frivolous, who are active in deeds of charity, who refrain from sex except with those joined to them in marriage, or those whom they rightfully possess – for then, they are free of all blame, whereas those who seek to go beyond that (limit) are indeed transgressors, who are faithful to their trusts and to their pledges, and who are diligent in their prayers. These shall be the heirs who will inherit Paradise; therein shall they abide. (23: 1–11)

Let us also reflect on the following hadith: Abu Hurayrah reports that the Prophet said: 'Seven types of people will be under God's shade on the Day when there is no shade other than His: a just ruler; a young person brought up attending to the worship of God; a person whose heart is inclined towards mosques; two people who love each other for God's sake: they uphold it when they meet and when they part; a man who is tempted by a woman who combines power with beauty, but he says: "I fear God"; a person who gives a *sadaqah* in secret, concealing it to the extent that his right hand does not know what his left hand has given; and a person who remembers God when alone and his eyes are tearful (in fear of Him).' (Related by al-Bukhari and Muslim)

Factors that strengthen a Muslim's conscience

God's Messenger (peace be upon him) highlights three factors that strengthen a Muslim's conscience and consolidate his piety. The first of these is early marriage or fasting. One of the positive and practical measures the Prophet encouraged to help Muslim men and women to overcome temptation is early marriage. If this is unavailable to a Muslim, then the Prophet advises such a person to resort to fasting, because it reduces the sexual urge. In either of these two courses, a person does not suffer the sort of suppression of desire that has adverse consequences. The Prophet says: "Young people, whoever of you can afford marriage, should get married, because marriage helps in lowering one's gaze (at women) and in maintaining chastity. Those who are unable to marry may fast, as fasting reduces desire." (Related by al-Bukhari and Muslim)

When a Muslim is married, he should follow a practice which the Prophet taught his Companions by word and deed. Jābir reports that 'God's Messenger (peace be upon him) saw a woman. He went to Zaynab, his wife, when she was dying a piece of leather. He had his business with her, then came out to meet his Companions. He said to them: "A woman comes in the image of a Satan and returns in the image of a Satan. If any of you sees a woman, let him go to his wife. This will stop what he experiences." (Related by Muslim) In a different version: 'Let him go to his wife; for she has the same as the other one.'

The second factor is the set of fine manners the Prophet urged be observed in mixed meetings between men and women. These manners prevent what excites temptation and limits natural attraction to the minimum. They help a person to steer a clean course of action. We devoted Chapter 2 in Volume 2 of this series to a detailed discussion of these manners.

The third factor is the collective responsibility of Muslim society. The Prophet (peace be upon him) makes clear that every Muslim is responsible for the Muslim community and he or she must always be alert to what such responsibility requires of them. God says in the Qur'an: 'The believers, men and women, are friends to one another: They enjoin what is right and forbid what is wrong.' (9: 71) Abu Sa'īd al-Khudrī reports that he heard God's Messenger say: 'Whoever of you sees an evil action should change it with his hand. If he is unable to do so, then with his tongue; and if he is unable to do even that, then with his heart. That is the weakest of faith.' (Related by Muslim)

Thus, a Muslim society remains alert to whatever occurs within it: it praises what is good and censures evil. It reminds the oblivious and educates the ignorant. Thus, society becomes a permanent watchguard, serving as one who reminds and educates, a means of deterrence, a factor of protection and a means of safety. It functions when an individual's or a group's conscience weakens and becomes complacent, overlooking the manners that must be observed in meetings between men and women.

Examples of an alert social role are found in some situations when the Prophet or his Companions showed the way to follow:

- ‘Abdullāh ibn ‘Abbās narrated: ‘Al-Faḍl (‘Abdullāh’s brother) was riding behind the Prophet when a woman from Khath‘am spoke to the Prophet. Al-Faḍl kept gazing at her and she looked at him. The Prophet kept turning al-Faḍl’s face to the other direction....’ (Related by al-Bukhari and Muslim)
- Khawāt ibn Jubayr said: ‘I came out of my tent and I saw some women chatting, and I liked them. I went back and took out my suitcase. I picked up a suit and put it on. I then went out and sat with them. God’s Messenger (peace be upon him) then came out and said: “I am God’s servant.” When I saw him, I felt agitated and did not know what to say. I then said: “Messenger of God, a camel of mine has run away and I am trying to find a rope for it.” He left me... Whenever he caught up with me during our march, he said: “Peace be to you, Abu ‘Abdullāh. What have you done about your runaway camel?”... I then thought: I must apologize to God’s Messenger... I said: “By Him who sent you with the message of the truth, no camel of mine ran away ever since I embraced Islam.” He said: “May God bestow mercy on you,” repeating it three times. He never said the same thing to me after that.’ (Related by al-Ṭabarānī)
- Umm Salamah narrated: ‘God’s Messenger (peace be upon him) visited me when Abu Salamah passed away. I had applied aloe vera drops to my eye. He asked me: “What is this, Umm Salamah?” I said: “It is aloe vera; it has no perfume.” He said: “It makes the face radiant. Therefore, apply it only at night.”’ (Related by al-Nasā’ī)
- Subay‘ah bint al-Ḥārith was married to Sa‘d ibn Khawlah, but he died during the Farewell Pilgrimage. Only a short while after that she gave birth to her child. When she regained her strength, she started to wear make-up expecting a proposal. Abu al-San‘bil ibn Ba‘kak came to her and said: “How come you are adorned expecting a proposal, hoping to get married? By God, you cannot get married before the

lapse of four months and ten days (after your husband's death)." Subay'ah said: 'When he said this to me, I put on my clothes in the evening and went to God's Messenger (peace be upon him) and I asked him about this. He told me that I had finished my waiting period when I gave birth and he left it up to me to get married if I wished.' (Related by al-Bukhari and Muslim)

- Abu Hurayrah saw a woman going to the mosque, and she had applied some perfume. He asked her: 'Where are you going, servant of the Almighty?' She said: 'To the mosque.' He asked her: 'And you have worn perfume for the mosque?' She said: 'Yes.' He said: 'I heard God's Messenger (peace be upon him) say: "Any woman who goes to the mosque after having worn perfume shall not have her prayer accepted until she has taken a bath."' (Related by Ibn Mājah)

The importance of resisting temptation, once again

The Prophet considered the suggestion of some of his Companions to emasculate themselves an evasion of facing and resisting temptation. By the same token, we may consider the extreme views of prohibiting the uncovering of women's faces and their meeting with men, in permissible situations, a similar evasion of facing and resisting temptation. When evasion is resorted to, many good benefits and interests are lost. Moreover, the person who resorts to evasion suffers weakness of personality and instability. By contrast, the resistance of temptation and facing up to it yield good benefits, strengthening and stabilizing one's personality.

Some Sufis abandon some permissible things so as to escape temptation. This may involve an effort of self-restraint, but it is an excessive type in the wrong place. Therefore, it yields nothing good. By contrast, self-restraint while doing what is permissible is healthy, moderate and certain to bring about good benefits.

Because facing and resisting temptation are highly important, we need to look at some examples of its different levels, as stated in the Sunnah.

Grade 1: Facing up to a very hard test, saying: 'I fear God':

Prophet Joseph provides the best example of such an attitude. God says about him: 'She in whose house he was living tried to seduce him. She bolted the doors and said, "Come." He said: "God protect me. Goodly has my master made my stay here. Those who do wrong come to no good."' (12: 23)

Abu Hurayrah reports that the Prophet said: 'Seven types of people will be under God's shade on the Day when there is no shade other than His: a just ruler... a man who is tempted by a woman who combines power with beauty, but he says: "I fear God."'

Grade 2: A man admires a pretty woman but resists and goes to his wife:

Jābir said that he heard the Prophet say: 'If any of you sees a woman and is attracted by her, he should go to his wife and have intercourse with her. That is enough to remove what he has experienced.' (Related by Muslim)

Grade 3: A man who looks once or several times, but he remembers or is reminded:

ʿAbdullāh ibn ʿAbbās narrated: "... A woman from Khathʿam spoke to the Prophet. Al-Faḍl kept gazing at her and she looked at him. The Prophet kept turning al-Faḍl's face to the other direction...." (Related by al-Bukhari and Muslim)

Grade 4: A man commits a minor offence, but then remembers and turns back in repentance:

Ibn Masʿūd reported that a man kissed a woman. He came to the Prophet (peace be upon him) and told him. God revealed the verse that says: "Attend to your prayers at both ends of the day and in the early watches of the night. Surely, good deeds erase evil ones." (11: 114) (Related by al-Bukhari and Muslim)

Grade 5: A man who sought to commit fornication, but at the point of action he is reminded of God and stops:

'Abdullāh ibn 'Umar narrated that God's Messenger (peace be upon him) said: 'Three people from a past community were walking together and then entered a mountain cave. A rock from the mountain fell over the entrance to their cave and blocked it. They said to each other: "Recall some good deeds you have done for God's sake and pray to God, appealing to Him by these. God may then clear it for you"... The second man said: "My Lord, I had a cousin whom I loved as dearly as any man could love a woman. I tried to get her but she refused me. Then she suffered from famine, and she came to me. I paid her one hundred and twenty dīnārs, on condition that she would let me have my way with her. She agreed. When I was about to have my way with her, she said: 'Servant of God! I do not allow you to open this seal except lawfully.' I stopped, unwilling to force her. I left her although she was the one I loved most. If You know that I did this only for Your sake, grant us an opening." God made an opening.' (Related by Muslim)

Grade 6: One who commits adultery but repents and seeks to be punished:

Buraydah narrated: 'The Ghāmidī woman came to the Prophet and said: "Messenger of God, I have committed adultery. Let me be cleansed."' (Related by Muslim)

Grade 7: One who commits adultery, repents and seeks God's cover:

Sa'īd ibn al-Musayyib reported that a man from the Aslam clan came to Abu Bakr and said that he committed adultery. Abu Bakr asked him: 'Have you mentioned this to anyone other than me?' He said:

'No.' Abu Bakr said to him: 'Then turn to God in sincere repentance and seek His cover. God accepts His servants' repentance.' (Related by Mālik)

The following scenario is related in al-Ṭabarī's commentary on the Qur'an whereby a man came to 'Umar and said: 'I had a daughter who was buried alive in pre-Islamic days, but I managed to rescue her before she died. She embraced Islam, but subsequently committed a grave sin. She took a blade to kill herself. I only reached her after she had cut some vein close to her throat. I treated her until she fully recovered. Then she repented well. Now I am receiving proposals of marriage with her. Should I tell the suitor of her past?' 'Umar said to him: 'Do you want to tell of her past? Do you expose what God has kept covered? By God, if you tell any person about her past, I shall make of you an example for the people of all regions. Give her in marriage like a chaste Muslim woman.'

Grade 8: One who raped a woman and escaped his chasers, but then confessed to save the one wrongly accused:

Wā'il al-Kindī reported that 'A woman was raped by a man as she was going to the mosque in the darkness at dawn. She appealed to a passer-by for help, but the rapist ran away. Then a group of people passed by her, and she appealed to them for help. They caught up with the one to whom she had appealed but the other (i.e. the rapist) managed to run away. They brought her the man they caught. He said to her: "I am the one who helped you, but the other has run away." They took him to God's Messenger (peace be upon him) who was told that the man raped her. They told him that they caught him running. He said: 'I was chasing the one who assaulted her, but these people caught me." She said: "He lies. He is the one who raped me." God's Messenger (peace be upon him) said: "Take him and stone him." A man stood up and said: "Do not stone him, but stone me instead. I was the one who committed the offence." Thus, three people were standing in front of God's Messenger (peace be upon him):

the rapist, the one who responded to her appeal and the woman. The Prophet said (to the one who raped her): "As for you, God has forgiven you." He also said good words to the one who responded to the woman's appeal for help. 'Umar said: "Shall we stone the one who admitted adultery"? The Prophet said: "No, because he turned to God in repentance." I think he said: "His repentance is such that it would have sufficed for the whole population of Madinah."' (Related by Ahmad)

Grade 9: One who yielded to Satan, becoming a prostitute, but her lingering compassion ensured God's forgiveness:

Abu Hurayrah reports that the Prophet said: 'A prostitute from among the Children of Israel saw a dog going around a well. He was almost dying of thirst. She took off her shoe and gave him a drink. (Another version says: She took off her shoe, tied it to her headcover and brought up some water for the dog) God forgave her her sin because of that.' (Related by al-Bukhari and Muslim)

Al-Fakhr al-Rāzī states the truth as he says: 'Every servant of God is too weak to be able to attend to all duties due to God in every area, hard as he may try. Everyone will fall short in one way or another. Therefore, all believers are recommended to turn to God in repentance, pray for His forgiveness and hope for success when they so repent and seek forgiveness.'

Turning to God in repentance is a means to earn God's forgiveness. However, God's Messenger (peace be upon him) has outlined several means through which a person can atone for any sin committed. These include:

Ablution: God's Messenger said: 'When a Muslim servant of God – or a believer – performs the ablution and washes his face, every sinful act he looked at with his eyes departs from his face with the water, or with the last drop of water.' (Related by Muslim)

Prayer: 'Suppose that one of you has a stream running just outside his house and he washes himself five times every day: will any dirt remain on his body?' People said: 'No dirt will remain.' The Prophet said: 'This is the same as the five obligatory prayers: with them God erases sins.' (Related by al-Bukhari)

Fasting: 'Whoever fasts in Ramadan, motivated by sincere faith and seeking God's reward, shall have all his past sins forgiven.' (Related by al-Bukhari)

Charity, enjoining right and forbidding evil: 'A man's indulgence with his family, children and neighbours is atoned for through prayer, charity, enjoining what is right and forbidding evil.' (Related by al-Bukhari)

Removing harmful objects from people's path: 'As a man was walking along a road, he found a thorny branch in the way. He picked it up and put it away. God thanked him for his action, forgiving him his sins.' (Related by al-Bukhari and Muslim)

Calamities: 'For whatever occurs to a Muslim of affliction, illness, worry, grief, injury or sadness, even if it be only a thorn in his side, God will forgive him some of his sins.' (Related by al-Bukhari)

The texts we have quoted put strong emphasis on God's forgiveness of people's sins. This may lead some people to be complacent with regard to the commitment of sin. It is important, therefore, to emphasize that the divine faith is solid and all its texts must be taken as constituting a single whole. The many texts we have cited speak of God's mercy and forgiveness, but there are many other texts that stress God's punishment and the suffering incurred by sinners. God says: 'Have fear of God, for God is severe in retribution.' (5: 2) 'Whatever the Messenger gives you, take it; and whatever he forbids you, abstain from it. Remain God-fearing; for God is severe in retribution.' (59: 7)

'Whoever repeats his offence, God will inflict His retribution on him. God is almighty, and He exacts retribution.' (5: 95)

Therefore, there should always be a balance between one's feelings of fearing God's punishment and hoping for His mercy. We must always maintain the thought that God is 'much-forgiving, ever-merciful' and that He is 'severe in retribution.' God says in the Qur'an: 'Tell My servants that I alone am much-forgiving, ever-merciful; and also, My punishment is indeed the most grievous suffering.' (15: 49-50) However, the most important point that the texts speaking of God's mercy emphasize is given in the following address that leaves no room for despair. A sinner who loses hope of God's mercy will see no path to follow other than persistence in sin. Thus, he becomes a prey to Satan. Hence God gives us this most hopeful address: 'Say: "[Thus speaks God]: You servants of Mine who have transgressed against their own souls! Do not despair of God's mercy: God forgives all sins; He alone is much-forgiving, ever-merciful."' (39: 53)

Important Objectives for the Moderate Approach to Cause Prevention

The importance of making things easy

Making things easy is an essential rule of the Islamic code of law, i.e. the Shariah. God says: 'God desires that you have ease. He does not desire that you be afflicted with hardship.' (2: 185) He also says: 'God has laid no hardship on you in anything that pertains to religion; the creed of your forefather Abraham.' (22: 78) God's Messenger (peace be upon him) said: 'Make things easy; not difficult.' 'Ā'ishah mentions: 'Whenever God's Messenger (peace be upon him) had to choose between two things, he chose the easier.'

This hadith highlights an important matter, namely, that the Prophet's guidance clearly points to choosing what is easier, not the harder, as some who give rulings always tend to express.

A clear Fiqh rule states: 'Hardship calls for concession.' That what is permissible is wide in scope ensures making things easier for people in all their affairs. By contrast, limiting the scope of the permissible makes things harder and leaves people in difficulty. Moderation in the implementation of cause prevention, which is clearly the preferred method of Islam, ensures that the scope of permissibility remains broad. It only narrows this scope in exceptional situations. Thus, it ensures making things easy, which is what God prefers. It is extremism that limits the scope and keeps it very narrow, as it prohibits many things that God, in His infinite wisdom, has permitted.

Every Muslim starts as innocent

The moderate approach to the rule of cause prevention emphasizes the starting point that considers every Muslim innocent, which means that a Muslim has an upright nature. It is this upright nature that makes religious duties applicable to every believer. God says: 'We indeed have created man in the finest form, then We brought him down to the lowest of the low, except for those who believe and do good deeds; for theirs shall be an unfailing recompense.' (95: 4-6) 'Man is born with a restless disposition: when misfortune befalls him, he is fretful; and when good fortune comes his way, he grows tight-fisted. Not so those who pray.' (70: 19-22)

Believers who attend to their prayers enjoy being created 'in the finest form', and they are well equipped to remain straight. They enjoy God's trust that they will obey His commandments and steer away from what He has forbidden. They are the truly God-fearing. Although believers may experience moments of weakness, the Wise Legislator, i.e. God, appreciates the fact that those who pray are straight and innocent. This is reflected in the fact that He allows many forms of women's participation in social life, including joining jihad campaigns when they give the fighters water to drink, tend the wounded and transport those who are ill. All these activities keep the women well involved, even though they may open ways for temptation. Yet, God the Legislator, permits these, acting on the basis that all Muslims, men and women, are innocent. Besides, such services are needed by Muslim armies.

God also permits a Muslim to look after the family of a fellow Muslim who is away on a jihad campaign. Indeed, Islam encourages this. Zayd ibn Khālid said that God's Messenger (peace be upon him) said: '... And whoever succeeds a fighter for God's cause, attending well to his affairs (adding in Muslim's version: looking after his family], is himself a fighter.' (Related by al-Bukhari and Muslim) Needless to say that 'looking after another's family' involves interaction with a woman whose husband is away and may remain so for a long time. This provides ample opportunity for temptation. Yet, in His infinite wisdom, the Legislator approves and encourages such succession and looking after another man's family, trusting to the Muslims integrity. Thus, the woman concerned can have what she needs without difficulty, and the spirit of cooperation and unity within the Muslim community is enhanced. Since this situation involves a greater trust in a Muslim's integrity, the punishment is greater should there be a case of betrayal of trust. The Prophet highlights that being unfaithful to an absent fighter with his wife is an abhorrent offence that merits very severe punishment. He said: 'The sanctity of jihad fighters' wives to those who stay behind is the same as the sanctity of their own mothers. If a man who stays behind and undertakes looking after a fighter's family, then acts with infidelity shall stand face-to-face with him on the Day of Judgement. He (i.e. the fighter) shall take whatever he wants of the other's good deeds. What do you think (he will take]?'

If the approach of moderation to the question of cause prevention indicates trust in the innocence of Muslims, a very strict approach negates such innocence and betrays distrust of Muslims, as though they are out and about to attack every woman they meet. By contrast,

God teaches us to trust the Muslim community and to think well of Muslims. In reference to the Story of Falsehood,[6] God says: 'When you heard it, why did not the believers, men and women, think the best of themselves, and say: 'This is a blatant falsehood.' (24: 12)

Highlighting the importance of the permissible

As we have noted, the moderate approach to the implementation of the rule of cause prevention gives us a clear idea of the importance of what is permissible under Islamic law. The Shariah is not limited to obligation and prohibition. As Muslims fulfil their obligations and steer away from prohibitions, they need to go at ease into the area of what is permissible, which stretches over a wide expanse. It is important, therefore, to maintain all three areas, as they have been stated by God.

All duties are positive actions. A positive action may be hard, but it contributes something new to man and life. Indeed, it may attain the grade of creativity. Therefore, we look at all obligations as profits to man and human life. Their rates of profit are commensurate to the degree of sincerity in addressing them purely to God, and to how well they are done. Since some people are weak and others strong, God says in reference to obligations: 'God does not charge a soul with more than it can bear.' (2: 286)

Forbidden things are foul and evil. They corrupt life. In reference to His Messenger (peace be upon him), God says: 'He forbids them all that is foul.' (7: 157) These are outlined and well-known. God's Messenger tells the truth as he says: 'God's protected area on earth is what He has forbidden.' This means that the forbidden part of

6. The Story of Falsehood refers to the false accusation levelled by some hypocrites against 'Ā'ishah.

God's earth is narrow and limited, while God's earth is expansive. As we have said, doing one's duties yields new profit for man every day. Likewise, steering away from what is forbidden yields more profit, as it gives man renewed purity.

What is permissible includes all the good things in this life. God says: 'He makes lawful to them the good things of life.' (7: 157) All the good things, numerous as they are, are lawful to mankind. This means that everyone has broad freedom to partake of good things. We must not restrict what God has kept unrestricted, except when they are contaminated by filth. Sexual pleasure is wholesome when it is within the bounds of marriage, but it is a form of robbery when it is adulterous. Grape and date drinks are fine, but alcoholic drinks are foul. Capital investment with effort and trade gives fine profit, but usury is abhorrent exploitation.

Let us reflect on the following Qur'anic verses. All of them highlight the serious negative effects of forbidding what is permissible:

- Stricter prohibition is a divine punishment for wrongdoing: God says: 'So, then, for the wrongdoing of the Jews did We forbid them some of the good things of life which had been formerly allowed to them; and, indeed for their turning away often from God's path, and for their taking usury although it had been forbidden to them, and their wrongful devouring of other people's property. We have prepared for the unbelievers among them painful suffering.' (4: 160–161)
- God, the Exalted, censures the prohibition of what is lawful: He says: 'Say, "Who is there to forbid the beauty which God has produced for His servants, and the wholesome means of sustenance?" Say, "They are [lawful] in the life of this world, to all who believe – to be theirs alone on the Day of Resurrection." Thus do We make Our revelations clear to people of knowledge.' (7: 32) He also says: 'Prophet, why do you prohibit yourself something that God has made lawful to you

in your desire to please your wives? God is much-forgiving, ever-merciful.' (66: 1)

- Prohibiting what is permissible is an act of aggression against God and His law: 'Believers, do not forbid yourselves the good things God has made lawful to you. Do not exceed the bounds; God does not love those who exceed the bounds.' (5: 87) He also says: 'Losers indeed are those who, in their ignorance, foolishly kill their children and declare as forbidden what God has provided for them as sustenance, falsely attributing such prohibitions to God. They have gone astray and they have no guidance.' (6: 140)
- Prohibiting what is permissible is akin to associating partners with God: God says: 'Those who associate partners with God will say: "Had God so willed, neither we nor our fathers would have associated any partners with Him; nor would we have declared anything as forbidden." In like manner did those who have lived before them deny the truth, until they came to taste Our punishment. Say: Have you any certain knowledge which you can put before us? You follow nothing but conjecture, and you do nothing but guess.' (6: 148) He also says: 'Those who associate partners with God say, "Had God so willed, neither we nor our forefathers would have worshipped any other than Him, nor would we have declared anything forbidden without a commandment from Him." Those before them said the same. Are the messengers bound to do anything other than to clearly deliver the message?' (16: 35)
- Prohibiting what is permissible and permitting what is forbidden are similar acts of aggression against God's law: God says: 'Say: Do but consider all the means of sustenance that God has bestowed on you! Some of it you then made unlawful, and some lawful. Say: Has God given you leave to do so, or do you fabricate lies against God?' (10: 59) He also says: 'Do not say – for any false thing you may utter with your tongues – that "This is lawful and this is forbidden", so as to attribute your

> lying inventions to God. Indeed those who attribute their lying inventions to God will never be successful.' (16: 116)

There is no doubt that prohibiting what is permissible represents a serious offence against God's law. However, it may be asked: why do we repeatedly mention the prohibition of the permissible whilst not similarly reiterating permission of the forbidden? In answer, we say that permitting what is prohibited and forbidding what is permissible are equal acts of aggression against God's law and deviation from the straight path. The difference between the two is only in the attitude of devout, religious people to them.

It is rarely the case that religious people mistakenly consider a prohibited act lawful. If it occurs, it is soon realized, and the truth becomes apparent. Thus, believers will reject it and go back to the straight path. By contrast, prohibiting what is permissible mostly, if not always, lingers on. As time passes, the prohibition is consolidated and the permissibility appears to have been abrogated by a divine decree. Alternatively, the permissibility may appear as having never existed in the first place.

In what way does the prohibition of what is permissible represent a danger to the divine law? It is often confused with deceptive false claims, such as the claim of drawing closer to God and earning more reward, or the claim of steering away from what is doubtful, or the claim that it is an act of cause prevention and steering away from temptation. The Prophet emphatically censured the claim of increasing one's reward by refraining from what is permissible. We cited the hadith that mentions three of his Companions who thought that his voluntary worship was too little for them. He disapproved of what they intended to do and said to them: 'Whoever turns away from my practice (i.e. my Sunnah) does not belong to me.' Likewise, he most strongly censured the claim of steering away from what is doubtful. He said: 'Why do some people disdain to do what I myself do?' Taking his cue from this hadith, Imam al-Shawkānī said: 'Abandoning what is permissible is not an act of piety.'

However, some people may be confused concerning the meaning of the hadith that says: 'That which is lawful is plain and that which is unlawful is plain. In between the two there are doubtful matters which many people do not know. Whoever avoids doubtful matters clears himself in regard to his religion and his honour.' (Related by al-Bukhari and Muslim) Some people misunderstand the hadith and they tend to put many things in this category of 'doubtful', thus removing these from what is permissible. They do so, despite the fact that the hadith says: 'In between the two there are doubtful matters which many people do not know.' This means that these doubtful matters have clear rulings which are well known to a small number of people, i.e. to scholars. Thus, such matters appear doubtful to many people at some time or another. When they appear so, whoever is in doubt about them should refrain from them, but should also consult a scholar in order to remove the doubt. When this is done, the matter in question will take its place among what is permissible or among what is forbidden. It is no longer doubtful.

The third claim that is advanced to justify the prohibition of what is permissible is that it is an act of cause prevention and steering away from temptation. This is again false, because it does not comply with the conditions stated by scholars of legal theory to ensure that the rule of cause prevention is properly implemented. Such scholars establish a strict condition for the prohibition of what is permissible, which is that it leads to an evil that is certain to happen or that happens in most cases. However, some people tend to prohibit something permissible even if it rarely leads to evil. Such people tend to exaggerate the resulting evil and do not try to weigh up the benefit of the deed against the harm that may result from it so as to choose whether to allow it or not.

Islam is keen to protect what is permissible from any aggression that changes its ruling from permissibility to prohibition or reprehension. Maintaining the broadness of what is permissible is important because it enables man to benefit by the freedom God has granted him and it also ensures that God's law remains easy to follow, which encourages people to implement it. Both purposes enhance obedience of God and encourage people to embrace Islam in large number. By contrast, an extreme attitude, which forbids what God has made permissible, restricts man's freedom and distorts the image of God's law, thus turning people away from it. This is, in essence, disobedience of God and turning people away from the divine faith. Stressing the same meaning, Shaykh Yusuf al-Qaradawi says: 'Exaggeration, particularly stressing the prospect of doom, often leads to adverse psychological results. Those who resort to such exaggeration often lead people to turn away from God and form a negative concept of Him.'

Islam frees the divine, true faith from all false appearance, particularly the stigma of subjugating man. It is such stigma that turns rational and wise people away from religion. Therefore, the Islamic code of law removes the shackles of prohibiting the good things of life. Such prohibition means withholding God's mercy from people and leading them into submission to soothsayers and false claimers of religious knowledge, in the hope that they will remove some of these shackles of prohibition, even by resort to trickery or deception.

To sum up: exaggerated prohibition is an age-old trick leading people into error and disobedience of God. Steering away from such exaggeration and maintaining the broad area of permissibility has always been the right approach that helps people to remain on the right course of obedience of God. Therefore, Islam takes care to set a number of duties to maintain its concept of permissibility and its broad application. Here are the most important of these duties:

Duty 1: A Muslim must believe that Islamic law establishes permissibility

God says in the Qur'an: 'He makes lawful to them the good things of life and He forbids them all that is foul.' (7: 157) God's Messenger (peace be upon him) says: 'What is lawful is whatever God has stated in His Book as lawful and what is forbidden is whatever God has stated in His Book as forbidden. Whatever He has chosen not to mention belongs to what He has permitted.' (Related by al-Tirmidhī)

Some scholars of Fiqh methodology consider permissibility a religious requirement, in the sense that one should believe that God has established it. Abu Isḥāq al-Isfarāyīnī, a distinguished Shāfiʿī scholar, considered 'the permissible' a duty, because believing in its permissibility is a duty. Imam al-Ghazālī said: 'It may be asked: Does "the permissible" come under duty, and is it one of the duties? We answer that if a duty means requiring what needs effort, then this does not apply to what is permissible. On the other hand, if it means knowing what the Shariah has permitted and left open, then it is a duty. Moreover, if it means the requirement to believe that it is part of the Shariah, then we are so required, not by the fact of permissibility but by the essential act of believing.'

Duty 2: Explaining the permissible to people, by word and deed, and taking care not to confuse it with what is reprehensible or forbidden

- Muhammad ibn al-Munkadir narrated: 'Jābir offered prayers wearing a lower garment which he tied in the back, while he had other garments on the hanger nearby. Someone said to him: "Would you offer prayers wearing only one garment?" He answered: "I have done this so that someone like you, bereft of knowledge, should see me. (Another version says: I wanted some ignorant people like you see me). How many of us had two garments during the Prophet's lifetime?"' (Related by al-Bukhari)

Imam Ibn Ḥajar said: 'Jābir's purpose was to show that it is permissible to offer prayers wearing only one garment, although wearing two garments (i.e. upper and lower garments) is better. What he seems to imply is: I have done this on purpose to show that it is permissible, so that an ignorant person will follow my example, or will question me and I will then inform him that it is acceptable.'

☙ Nazzāl ibn Sabrah narrated that "Alī ibn Abi Ṭālib offered the Ẓuhr Prayer, then he sat in the main square of Kufah to attend to people's needs. He remained so until it was the time for 'Aṣr Prayer. He was then brought some water. He drank of it and washed his face, hands, head and feet. He then stood up and drank what was left of the water in the standing position. He then said: "Some people dislike drinking and standing, but the Prophet did what I have just done."' (Related by al-Bukhari)

Imam Ibn Ḥajar said: 'This hadith of what 'Alī did highlights the need for a scholar, who notes that people refrain from something which he knows to be permissible to explain to them the right ruling. If such explanation is neglected for a long time, some people may begin to think that this action is forbidden. If a scholar fears this, he should make sure that he informs people of the right ruling, even though he is not asked about it. If he is asked, the duty is even more binding on him.'

Al-Shāṭibī puts the question of the need to explain religious rulings by word, then by deed, most succinctly, so that people do not become confused. This equally applies to explaining what is recommended so that it is not confused with what is obligatory. It further applies to explaining the discouraged so that it is not confused with what is forbidden. Likewise, what is permissible should be explained so that it is not confused with either the recommended or the discouraged. Thus, God's law continues to hold the last word, without addition or omission. Imam al-Shāṭibī said:

When deeds are added to verbal statements, they are more likely to be heeded and emulated than verbal advice on its own. Therefore, deeds become necessary from a person whose example is followed. Indeed, in this sense we may say that for anyone who is emulated and able to speak and explain, it is obligatory that he should examine all what he says and does. This applies equally to all that is duty, recommended, permissible, discouraged or prohibited. The words and deeds of such a person are considered in two ways. The first is that he himself is one of the people to whom the code of law applies. Therefore, all five rulings are applicable to him. The second is that what he says, does or approaches are considered as statements and explanations of what God has legislated. His position as such means that all his words and deeds are either duties or forbidden. There is no third category. In this sense, he is a source of information, and providing information is obligatory. If the matter in question is something that is done or said, it must, generally speaking, be done. If it is something which is not to be done, its omission is obligatory, as will presently be explained, by God's help. This means that doing it is forbidden. This is all applicable to the one who is emulated or followed: it becomes necessary when there is need for explanation, either because people are unaware of the ruling concerning doing or leaving something, or they believe or are thought to believe the opposite of the correct ruling.

What needs to be done: this is explained by doing it, or by words that confirm the deed if that deed is obligatory or recommended and its ruling is unknown. If it may be thought to be a duty but is, in fact, recommended, then it is explained by omission, or by words that are added to omission. Such examples of omission are to abstain from offering the sacrifice at the time of Eid al-Aḍḥā, or the omission of fasting six days from Shawwāl. On the other hand, if the deed is thought not to be recommended, or thought to be ignored, then its explanation is by doing it and continuing to do it as the case may require. This is what needs to be done in the case of recommended practices that have been forgotten or ignored these days.

What needs to be omitted: this is explained by refraining from doing it, or by words that confirm abstention from it if it is forbidden or discouraged and its ruling is unknown. If it is discouraged but may be thought to be forbidden and its explanation is better shown by deed, then it must be done in the least and easiest way.

In general, what is needed in this respect is to provide proper and full explanation that helps people to steer away from error and deviation and bring them back to the straight path. Studying the practice of the devout early Muslims confirms what we have stated. It is imperative to give this explanation of all five rulings or some of them, so that their purpose is clear. We seek God's help in all this...

The recommended: Its establishment as something recommended means that it must not be equated, either by word or deed, with what is obligatory, in the same way as these two are not equated in belief. If they are treated equally by word or deed, then this must be in a way that does not encroach on belief. This is explained in several ways:

1. To believe that the duty and recommended are equal is wrong, according to the unanimous view of scholars. This means that a person considers something to be a duty when it is not. If words or a deed leads to the equation of the two, then distinction between them must be provided, and

this can only be done by verbal explanation, and by action that shows such distinction. Such action means refraining from consistently doing what is recommended. Such occasional omission is an aspect of its being recommended, not obligatory.

2. The Prophet (peace be upon him) was sent as a guide who explains to people what was revealed to them. He did this in many situations.
3. The Prophet's Companions who clearly understood this essential principle of the Islamic code of law, i.e. the Shariah, and were leaders to be followed, were keen to take such precaution. They omitted certain things and showed such omission, so as to show that although these were good and desirable things, their omission is not wrong. Ḥudhayfah ibn Usayd said: 'I witnessed that Abu Bakr and 'Umar did not offer the sacrifice, fearing that people might think that it is obligatory.'
4. Leading Islamic scholars generally continued this practice, although they differed in detail. Mālik and Abu Ḥanīfah expressed discouragement of the fasting of six days from Shawwal, for the above-stated reason, although encouragement to undertake such fasting is confirmed. They feared that such fasting would become an addition to fasting during Ramadan. Al-Qarāfī said: 'This occurred in the case of some non-Arabs.' Imam al-Shāfi'ī expressed a similar view regarding the sacrifice. He cited what we mentioned of the Prophet's Companions who did not do it as evidence and justification. Many other examples are cited from Mālik. 'Cause prevention' is an essential rule according to him, and it is applicable to acts of worship as also people's normal actions.

All this evidence clearly shows that drawing a distinction between what is obligatory and what is recommended is religiously required if the two utterances or two deeds are equal. Such distinction is certainly required from everyone who is considered a leader to be emulated, in the same way that distinguishing them in belief is certainly required. That the recommended is well-established means that doing it is not treated in the same way as doing what is obligatory.[7] Likewise, its clear establishment means that it is not treated in the same way as some permissible things in their omission, without explanation...

Permissible things become well established as permissible by not equating them with either the recommended or the discouraged. If they are equated with the recommended by consistently doing them in a particular manner, people may think that they are recommended... Likewise, if they are equated with the discouraged by omission, people may think that they are discouraged... Discouraged things become well established as discouraged when they are neither equated with the forbidden nor with the permissible. If they are equated with the forbidden, people may start to think them forbidden. As time passes, people with little knowledge may believe that refraining from them is obligatory. It should not be said that to do such an action means doing what is discouraged, when this is reprehensible. In response to such argument we say: setting things clearly is more important. A definitely prohibited action may be done if doing it serves a clear and needed interest.

7. This is confirmed by the following report given by Masrūq: 'When 'Abdullāh (ibn Mas'ūd) left, we stayed on and people would check their recitation. When we rose to leave, we would pray (the recommended sunnah). 'Abdullāh was informed of this. He said to us: "are you obliging people to do what God has not made obligatory to them? When you pray, they may think such prayer to be obligatory. If you are keen to offer such prayer, do it at home."' – Author's note.

Limitless is God in His glory! Scholars of legal theory were magnificent in their efforts to keep all rulings absolutely clear and free of confusion. They made it clear that what is permissible must be distinguished from what is discouraged. To my mind, keeping the permissible clearly distinguished from what is forbidden is more imperative. There is no doubt that forbidding what is permissible is the same as permitting what is forbidden. God's Messenger tells the truth as he says: 'The one who forbids what is permissible is the same as one who permits what is forbidden.' As mentioned earlier, the difference is that permitting what is forbidden is often clearly and easily known. This is for two reasons: (1) what God has forbidden is small in number and can easily be known to people, and (2) the efforts of transgressors are weak, and their attempts are easily discovered. Moreover, the forbidden often has a foul smell attached to it. By contrast, evil as forbidding the permissible is, it is often supported by some false claims that are unfortunately promoted by good intentions. It should be clear to us that forbidding the permissible is the same as permitting the forbidden in the way that both represent a clear offence and an act of aggression on God's authority. In other words, there is no difference between one who usurps a portion of God's authority by trespassing on God's bounds on earth, and another who usurps a portion of God's authority by forbidding some of the beauty which God has produced for His servants. This despite the fact that the area within those bounds is small while the beauty is extensive and broadly spread.

Both types are wicked acts of aggression. God says: 'Believers, do not forbid yourselves the good things God has made lawful to you. Do not exceed the bounds; God does not love those who exceed the bounds.' (5: 87) Both are negations of rulings God has set in place. God says: 'Do they desire to be ruled by the law of pagan ignorance? But for those who are firm in their faith, who can be a better law-giver than God?' (5: 50) Both are distortions of the good life God wants people to lead. God says: 'Say: Who is there to forbid the beauty which God has produced for His servants, and the wholesome means of sustenance?' (7: 32)

Permitting what is forbidden is an aggression on the purity of human life, while forbidding what is permissible is an aggression on its beauty. God wants human life to be beautiful, just as much as He wants it to be pure. However, transgressors (may God enable them to reform) are not keen to maintain its purity, whilst those who follow a hard line (may God help them mend their ways) do not like its beauty. However, human life will never be right unless it adheres to what God wants it to be. If it transgresses, it remains awry and distorted, leading the transgressors to their doom and putting the extremists into difficulty and hardship. God who knows His creation has given them a law reflecting His infinite wisdom. He sent His Messenger to shed His light on human life. He describes the believers as 'those who follow the Messenger, the unlettered Prophet whom they shall find described in the Torah and the Gospel that are with them. He commands them to do what is right and forbids them to do what is wrong, and makes lawful to them the good things of life and forbids them all that is foul. He lifts from them their burdens and the shackles that weigh upon them. Those, therefore, who believe in him, honour and support him, and follow the light that has been bestowed from on high through him shall indeed be successful.' (7: 157)

In His infinite wisdom, God has willed to remove from the community of Prophet Muhammad (peace be upon him) the shackles that used to burden earlier communities. He has willed that His final code of law should be easy and simple. This establishes an important and essential religious rule, which is the preference of what makes things easier for people. God tells the truth as He says: 'God desires that you have ease. He does not desire that you be afflicted with hardship.' (2: 185)

CHAPTER II

Scholars' Statements about the Rule of Cause Prevention

- One: From Books of Legal Theory
- Two: From the Writings of Scholars

One: From Books of Legal Theory

1. From *al-Furūq* by Imam Ahmad ibn Idris al-Qarāfī

Cause prevention refers to stopping the means that lead to error and sin. When an action, which is not foul in itself, leads to foul results, Mālik prohibits such an act in many instances. Cause prevention is not peculiar to the Mālikī School, as many Mālikī scholars imagine. Causes may be divided into three sets: (1) What the entire Muslim community agree must be prevented and disallowed in every way, such as digging wells on people's roads, because it leads to their fall and death; (2) What the entire Muslim community agree not to prevent, because it is a means that should not be prevented or stopped, such as trying to prevent the growing of grapes so that they are not used to brew wine. No one agrees to this. Likewise, disallowing the building of homes close to each other, in order to prevent adultery, and (3) A set on which scholars hold different views as to whether they should be prevented or not. One example is the case of sales tied to a specific time term, such as a person selling something for ten pounds with the payment being deferred for a month, then buying it back for five pounds, before the end of the month. According to Mālik, such a person now pays five pounds, but then takes ten at the end of the month. This is akin to lending five and being repaid ten after a period of time, with the loan being given in the form of a sale. Mālik says this is not permissible, thereby preventing the cause of a usurious transaction. On the other hand, al-Shāfiʿī looks only at the form of sale and treats the transaction in its apparent form, making it permissible. Similarly, scholars differ regarding the ruling on staring at women: should it be prohibited because it may lead to adultery?

In *Tahdhīb al-Furūq*: Ibn al-ʿArabī says in his book *al-Aḥkām*: The rule concerning the cause that must be prevented from the religious point of view applies to any permissible act that leads to something clearly stated as forbidden, not to any type of wrong... Every feared thing which God has left to the individual and his conscience may not be described as a means that leads to a forbidden thing so as to rule it as disallowed.

2. From *Iʿlām al-Muwaqqiʿīn* by Imam Ibn al-Qayyim

What can be said about this perfect code of law which has attained the pinnacles of wisdom, benefit and perfection? Whoever looks at its principles and details realizes that God has prevented the causes that lead to what is forbidden by forbidding these causes and warning against them. A 'cause' refers to what leads to something.

An act or speech that leads to harm is of two types: the first is that it is something meant to lead to such harm, such as drinking alcohol which leads to drunkenness; casual accusation which leads to fabrication, and fornication which leads to confused lineage, etc. These are deeds and speeches that lead to such types of harm, and they do not have any different apparent result. The second type is of things meant to lead to something permissible or desirable, but this result is taken as a means to what is forbidden, either deliberately or unintentionally. Examples of the first type include a person who arranges a marriage contract in order to make it lawful for the woman to remarry her former husband,[8] or a person who enters into a sale contract intending it as a cover for a usurious deal. Examples of the second type include someone who offers a voluntary prayer during the time when prayer is discouraged, without having a particular cause allowing it, or one who hurls verbal abuse on the deities of polytheists in their presence, or one who offers his prayer facing a grave, etc.[9]

Besides, this type of cause includes two kinds: the first is where benefit of the deed is greater than its harm, while the second results in harm that is greater than its benefit. Thus we have four categories: (1) An action that leads to harm. (2) An action that is meant for what is permissible but used with the intention to cause what is foul. (3) An action that is meant for what is permissible and not intended to cause what is foul; but it causes it in most cases and its harm is greater than its benefit, and (4) An action meant for what is permissible but may lead to something foul, and its benefit is greater than the harm it may cause. We cited examples of the first two categories. Examples of the third category include prayer at times of discouragement, reviling the deities of other people in their presence, a widow adorning herself during her waiting period, and similar matters. Of the fourth

8. This is the case of a woman who has been divorced three times by her husband. She cannot be reunited with him in marriage until she has married someone else, with the marriage intended to last for life. If her new husband dies or divorces her, she can remarry her former husband. However, someone who has divorced his wife three times may regret this and want to be reunited with her. He may arrange with someone to marry her for one night and then divorce her so that the two can be reunited. This is forbidden, and this arranged marriage is invalid.
9. Voluntary prayer is desirable except at certain times during the day, unless there is valid reason for offering them at that time. Likewise, facing a grave when praying is disallowed, because it gives the appearance of worshipping the person buried in the grave. Muslims are commanded not to revile the deities worshipped by other people. If one does this in front of those who worship them, this leads to conflict and possible trouble.

category, examples include looking at a woman whom one intends to marry, or one for whom a man is standing as a witness, or one with whom a person is dealing. Other examples include performing at the time when prayer is discouraged, some acts of worship that are recommended for a reason, and declaring the word of truth in the presence of a tyrannical ruler, etc. The Islamic Shariah makes this last category permissible or desirable or a duty, according to the degree of benefit expected from it. It also prevents the first category, ruling it either reprehensible or forbidden, according to the degree of harm it causes. There remain the second and third categories and whether they are permissible or not. There are, then, several aspects that require disallowing them.

Imam Ibn al-Qayyim provides 99 reasons as evidence confirming that the Islamic code of law disallows categories 2 and 3. We will quote only those which are relevant to the prevention of women's temptation.

> Reason 2. God says: 'Let them not swing their legs in walking so as to draw attention to their hidden charms.' (24: 31) Swinging their legs while walking is permissible in the first place, but here it is disallowed because it may let men hear the sound of their anklets when they do so, and this may arouse their desire.
>
> Reason 11. The Prophet prohibited that a man be alone with a woman in an enclosed place, even for the purpose of teaching her the Qur'an. He also prohibited travelling alone with her, even for performing the hajj or visiting her parents. This is to prevent what may be a cause for temptation.
>
> Reason 12. God orders men to lower their gaze, even though they look at the beauty of creation and this may

lead to contemplation of the excellence of God's creation. This order is to prevent what may be a cause of arousal that leads to what is forbidden.

Reason 53. The Prophet told women who pray with men in the mosque that when they stand up after prostration, they should delay raising their heads. This is to prevent them seeing the men's *'awrah*, if their lower garments are short. This is explained in the relevant hadith.

Reason 57. The Prophet ordered women who go out to the mosque not to wear perfume or smell of incense because this is a cause that excites men's desire. A woman's fine scent, adornment and charms make her more attractive. Therefore, the Prophet ordered women to go out well covered, wearing no perfume, and to stand behind the rows of male worshippers. He further ordered them not to say *Subḥān Allah* if they want to alert the imam during prayer. Instead, a woman should clap with the inside of her one hand over the back of the other. All these measures are advised as cause prevention and protection from evil and harm.

Reason 58. The Prophet prohibited a woman from describing another woman to her husband as though he is looking at her. This is a clear case of cause prevention. It protects the husband from feeling an inclination towards that woman as he may imagine her shape. The scenario of a person falling in love through mere description is not uncommon.

Reason 59. The Prophet ordered people not to sit by the roadside, because it is a cause of looking at what is forbidden. When his companions said that they could not dispense with this, he said: 'Then give the road its right.'

He named that as 'lowering the gaze, prevention of harm and returning greetings.'

Reason 60. The Prophet prohibited a man from spending the night at a woman's home unless he is her husband or a close relative who is forbidden to marry her. This is only because staying overnight at a stranger woman's home is a cause that may lead to what is forbidden.

Reason 63. The Prophet ordered that children's beds are separated, with no boy sleeping with a girl in the same bed, because this may be a means for Satan to tempt them into forbidden contact, particularly if this were to continue for some time. A man may touch a woman unaware and unintentionally during sleep if she is sleeping next to him. This is one of the most refined forms of cause prevention.

Reason 66. Women are not allowed to travel alone. A woman is required to be accompanied by a relative who is forbidden to marry her, or by her husband. Her being alone, away from home, may make her vulnerable to wicked designs.

Reason 82. Islam prohibits self-exultation about sex, because it may encourage some people to do the same. Some men may not be married and they may slip into what is forbidden. Therefore, those who boast about their sins are deprived of God's forgiveness, because their listeners may be encouraged to emulate them and this leads to the spread of sin in ways known only to God.

Imam Ibn al-Qayyim concludes this chapter on cause prevention with the following comment: 'The area of cause prevention is one quarter of obligation, which is of two types: an order to do and a prohibition from doing. The order is of two categories: one is required by itself and the other is required as a means to what is needed. The prohibition is also of two categories: either the prohibited thing is itself foul or it is a means leading to what is foul. As such, the prevention of causes that lead to what is forbidden is one quarter of the religion.'

This long discussion by Ibn al-Qayyim gives us the following conclusion:

1. Two conditions must be met before we can stop a permissible action. The first is that such action leads to what is foul, and this occurs often, not rarely. The other condition is that the foul result is greater than its likely benefit. It must not be the opposite. When these two conditions are met, the prevention of the cause must not be a categorical prohibition: it ranges between the discouraged and the prohibited, according to the nature of the foul result.
2. If the action leads to something foul but its benefit is greater than such foul result, the Shariah does not only consider the action permissible, but may also make it desirable or a duty, depending on the importance of its benefit.
3. The Islamic code of law establishes rulings that prevent actions that are normally permissible. These are prevented because they often lead to sexual temptation. They frequently lead to foul results. Some of these rulings are outlined in the 11 reasons we have quoted. Since Islamic law has, thus, prevented the causes of sexual temptation, we believe that we should accept these rulings and treat them as sufficient. We must not add to them other actions that are permissible. Nor must we prohibit such other actions under the pretext of cause prevention, unless new circumstances and developments occur which meet the above two conditions and were not present at the time of revelation.

3. From *al-Muwāfaqāt* by Imam al-Shāṭibī

Six:[10] Actions that rarely lead to foul results. These remain permissible, because when benefit is the more likely result, the rarer outcome is not taken into consideration. The fact is that normally, there is no beneficial action that is free from some negative aspect. In Islamic law, consideration is given to the preponderance of the benefit. The rare disadvantage is discarded.

Seven: Actions that are thought to lead to foul results, which means that we think that they most probably lead to such results. This is open to different views. That they are originally permissible and we are free to do them is clearly apparent as explained under Six above. If the harm or the foul result are thought to occur... then acting on this thinking is the weightier option for several reasons. One of these is that in practical matters, thoughts are treated as clear knowledge. Hence, it appears to be the right course of action to take...

Eight: When the foul result occurs often but it is found neither in the majority of cases nor rarely. This may be confusing and needs careful consideration. The essential ruling here is the continuity of its being permissible, as this is the view of the Shāfiʿī School and others. Moreover, here we have neither clear knowledge nor thought of the likelihood of the foul result. It is merely a question of a probable result that may or may not occur. There is no circumstantial evidence to make either result more probable. That harm or a foul result is probably intended cannot be treated as definite intention, because of the presence of various aspects such as unawareness of the possible foul outcome.

Imam al-Shāṭibī also speaks about a different question related to scholarly reasoning, i.e. *ijtihād*. He says:

---

10. As the author is including here a quotation from Imam al-Shāṭibī, he states it with the same numbering of the original.

> Looking at the outcome of deeds is certainly required and important, whether the deeds are consistent with these or not. A scholar does not give a ruling of permissibility or prohibition of any deed done by a Muslim until he has looked at the outcome of that deed. The deed may be permissible because of a benefit that attends on it or a harm that it prevents, yet it may lead to an outcome that is contrary to its intention. Alternatively, a deed may be prohibited because of the harm it produces or the benefit that it blocks, yet it may lead to a different outcome. If the first type of deed is ruled as always permissible, the benefit that it gives may lead to an equal or greater harm. This is a reason to prevent a general ruling of permissibility. The same applies to giving a general rule of prohibition in the second type. The prevention of the harm it causes may lead to an equal or greater harm. Therefore, it is wrong to give a general ruling of prohibition. This is a difficult area for a scholar who resorts to reasoning, but it is sweet and enjoyable because it pursues the objectives of the Shariah.

This quotation from Imam al-Shāṭibī gives us the following conclusions:

1. He agrees with Ibn al-Qayyim in preventing a permissible deed that leads to foul results in most cases, rather than rarely.
2. Under Eight above, al-Shāṭibī gives a third category of a deed that often leads to a foul result, but this is neither rare nor preponderant. Al-Shāfiʿī and other scholars are of the view that such deeds may not be disallowed, because 'it is merely a question of a probable result that may or may not occur. There is no circumstantial evidence to make either result more probable.'
3. He considers that the possibility that some people may resort to a permissible deed, such as social mixing between men

and women during shopping or study, in order to achieve a foul result cannot be treated like a deliberate intention. This possibility is discarded.

4. The harm or foul result that should be prevented must be equal to or greater than the benefit that accrues from the deed.
5. Al-Shāṭibī warns against the possibility that the prevention of a particular foul result may lead to a different result that is equally foul or even more so.

Two: From the Writings of Scholars

1. The cause leading to what is forbidden is not necessarily always forbidden

> ☙ 'Umar ibn al-Khaṭṭāb narrated: 'Feeling joyous, I kissed (my wife) when I was fasting. I said: "Messenger of God, I did today something very serious. I kissed when fasting." He said: "What do you say about rinsing your mouth with water when you are fasting?" I said: It is acceptable. He said: "Then, what?" (Related by Abu Dāwūd)

Al-Khaṭṭābī said: 'Rinsing one's mouth may lead to the water reaching one's throat and then going down to the stomach. This spoils fasting. Likewise, a kiss may lead to intercourse, which spoils fasting.'

This is further confirmed by the fact that some scholars are of the view that it is not permissible to wear perfume before entering into a state of consecration, or *iḥrām*, if its effect lingers after one starts consecration. They argue that wearing perfume may encourage sexual intercourse with one's wife, which is not permissible during consecration. However, an authentic hadith quotes 'Ā'ishah saying that she used to see the brightness of perfume on God's Messenger's forehead when he was in consecration. 'Ā'ishah is also quoted as saying: 'We used to apply perfumed musk on our faces before we started consecration. Then when we were in consecration, we may perspire and the musk may run over our faces. We were with God's Messenger (peace be upon him) and he did not prevent us.'

> Al-Sarakhsī says in *al-Mabsūṭ*: 'During the hajj, there are two releases from consecration. The first occurs when the pilgrim shaves his head and the other when he has performed the *ṭawāf* of *ifāḍah*. After shaving one's head, all that was forbidden during consecration becomes permissible, except sexual intercourse with one's spouse. Mālik (may God bestow mercy on him) said: 'except sexual intercourse and perfume...' He said: 'the use of perfume excites sexual desire. Therefore, like intercourse, it only becomes permissible after the *ṭawāf*.' Our argument is based on the hadith narrated by 'Ā'ishah: 'I used to apply perfume to God's Messenger (peace be upon him) at the time of *iḥrām* before he went into consecration, and at the time of his release before he performed the *ṭawāf* around the Ka'bah.'

What the Prophet said to 'Umar about kissing by a fasting person and his application of perfume before *iḥrām*, with its effect remaining after its start, and then its application before he performed the *ṭawāf* confirm that a cause to what is prohibited is only prevented when it leads to the wrong result in the majority of cases. It does not follow that such cause should always be prohibited.

2. When cause prevention requires action, it is a recommendation not an obligation, and when it requires abstention, it means discouragement, not prohibition

- Al-Bukhari relates the hadith narrated by Abu Saʿīd al-Khudrī that the Prophet said: 'Make sure not to sit by the roadside.' People said: 'Messenger of God, we cannot do without our meeting places where we sit and talk.' The Prophet said: 'Since you insist that you need to have these sittings, then give the road its right.' They asked: 'What is its right?' He said: 'That you lower your gaze, prevent harm, return greetings, enjoin what is right and forbid what is wrong.'

Imam Ibn Ḥajar says: 'It appears from the context of the hadith that the order not to sit by the roadside was meant as one of discouragement, so that those who so sit do not neglect their duties outlined in the hadith... The hadith serves as evidence in support of the view that cause prevention is merely to show the preferable option, not to give a strict order. The Prophet first orders refrain from sitting by the roadside, in order to prevent its possible neglect of duty. When his Companions said that they could not dispense with this, he outlined for them the purpose of the prevention. This makes clear that the first order of prohibition was merely for guidance to the better option.'

- Ibn Qudāmah writes in *al-Mughnī*: 'Al-Athram[11] said that he asked Ahmad ibn Ḥanbal about the action of a man who looks at his stepmother's leg or chest. Ahmad said: "I dislike it." He then added: "I dislike that a man looks at such parts of the body of his own mother or sister, and indeed any part

11. Abu Bakr Ahmad ibn Muhammad al-Athram was one of Imam Ahmad ibn Ḥanbal's disciples, and a great scholar in his own right.

that stirs desire." Abu Bakr al-Athram said: Ahmad's dislike of a person looking at his mother's leg or chest is a mere precaution. Such parts of the woman's body may stir desire. This means that it is discouraged, not forbidden.'

This means that when something is shunned for mere precaution, i.e. as a cause prevention, then it is only discouraged, not forbidden.

- In *al-Fatāwā al-Ḥadīthiyyah*, Ibn Ḥajar al-Haytamī comments on the Prophet's instruction to al-Shifā' bint 'Abdullāh: 'Teach her (i.e. Ḥafṣah) the supplication for the cure of *namlah* (which is skin inflammation on one's side) as you taught her to write.' He said: 'This serves as evidence that teaching writing to women is permissible. The maximum that can be said about its discouragement is merely to prevent its negative results.'[12]
- Al-Sarakhsī says in *al-Mabsūṭ*: 'It is reported that the Prophet was asked about a man who has sexual intercourse with his wife when both are in a state of consecration for hajj. He said: "They offer a sacrifice and continue their hajj. They must perform the hajj again the following year." The same is reported by the Prophet's Companions: 'Umar, Ibn Mas'ūd and 'Alī. However, they said that when the couple perform the hajj the following year, they should do it separately. In other words, each should take a different route. We say that the Prophet's Companions expressed this view by way of advice if the couple fear that they will encounter the same temptation. Their separation is not obligatory. Likewise, a young man is recommended not to kiss his wife during fasting if he fears that he may not be able to refrain from what is greater.'

12. The suggestion that there are any adverse results to teaching girls and women reading and writing is a claim that has no support whatsoever. – Author's note.

3. Needs and benefits must be considered when harm is being prevented

In his *al-Fatāwā*, Ibn Taymiyyah says:

- The extent of the harm that requires the prevention of something must be considered side by side with the need for it, which requires permissibility, or even desirability and obligation.
- Whatever is being prohibited on the basis of cause prevention is done only because such prohibition ensures weightier benefit... This is the reason for the prohibition of being alone with an unrelated woman in a secluded place, travelling with her and looking at her. These are prohibited because of the harm they may lead to. Thus a woman is disallowed from travel unless she is accompanied by her husband or a relative whom she is forbidden to marry... Such prohibition is stated because such situations lead to harm and foul results. What ensures a clear and weightier benefit does not lead to such harm or foul result.
- Whatever is discouraged, but allowed, does not remain discouraged if it is needed for an obligatory thing. Does it remain discouraged if it is needed for a desirable thing? Here we have a fluid situation because of the conflict between the foul element of discouragement and the benefit of the desirability. What we say is that it is sometimes encouraged if the benefit is greater, and discouraged if the harm is greater.
- One of the basic rules of Islamic law is that when benefit is opposed by harm, the greater one is adopted.

CHAPTER III

Later Generations Go Too Far in Cause Prevention

- Factors Leading to Extremism in the Application of the Rule of Cause Prevention

Later Generations Go Too Far in Cause Prevention

The rule of cause prevention means that a permissible matter becomes discouraged or even forbidden, if doing it leads to a foul result or temptation to sin. In itself, cause prevention is a solid rule, but its application is subject to a great deal of reasoning and beset by a broad difference of views. Thus, it tends to be a slippery area, beset by error. Whoever studies the books of Fiqh written in later generations, or reviews the way Muslims apply this rule will not fail to note how many errors have been committed in the application of this rule. Indeed, the rule is made to override many Islamic rulings. Thus, the life of Islamic society has been given a different colour to what it was during the Prophet's lifetime. Let us look at the following list of Islamic teachings:

- Islam encourages women to attend congregational prayers in the mosque;
- Islam orders women to attend the Eid Prayer;
- Islam recommends that the Imam devotes a special lesson for women;

- Islam recommends that after he has delivered the *khuṭbah* (i.e. the sermon) on Eid Day, the Imam addresses a special admonition to women in particular;
- Islam urges a man who intends to get married to see the woman he wants to marry;
- Islam orders women to learn what they need to follow their religion properly and to take care of their lives' needs;
- Islam requires women to enjoin what is right and speak out against what is wrong;
- Islam allows women to buy, sell and work to earn their living when they have no one to look after them, or to help their needy husbands;
- Islam permits women to accompany a Muslim army to tend the wounded and give drinks to thirsty fighters;
- Islam permits women to uncover their faces and hands when they go out, and
- Islam permits women to meet men, provided they observe Islamic standards of propriety.

However, all these have, at times, been disallowed citing the rule of cause prevention. Due to such exaggerated application of this rule, the life of the Muslim woman has been encumbered by a great variety of restrictions. Our predecessors might have had some reasons that justified such precautions, and whereby they thought such measures were right for their own time. Whether their decisions, based on their *ijtihad*, or reasoning, were right or wrong, no such decision is applicable for all times. Were it to apply for all time, it becomes a definitive religious ruling like God's own commandments. God knows His creation best, and He revealed to them His permanent and perfect code of law which safeguards life and honour. Therefore, if the additional and precautionary restrictions some people add are directly attached to man's nature, i.e. to every human being and their natural instincts, their attachment becomes an act of finding fault with God's legislation, while He, Mighty and Exalted, says: 'This day

I have perfected your religion for you.' (5: 3) It also constitutes a charge levelled at God's Messenger (peace be upon him), while he was the one who explained God's Book.

Those who advocate such permanent precautionary restrictions say that the first generation of Islam was the exception. They argue that it was the best of all generations and that the men and women who lived at that time attained a very high standard of good manners and fine morality. They make this exception in order not to appear to directly oppose the orders given by God and His Messenger. They overlook the fact that not every man in that society was like Abu Bakr, 'Umar, 'Uthmān or 'Alī, and not every woman was like 'Ā'ishah, Asmā' or Umm Sulaym (may God be pleased with all of them). There were in that society different groups, including hypocrites, Jews and desert Arabs who came to live in Madinah. It was a society that included the young and old, the strong and weak, and some of these were wise and rational while others were of limited intelligence. Nevertheless, Islam made its legislation clear and allowed women a broad area of freedom.

It is important to draw a distinction between the rulings clearly stated by Islam and the exceptional and temporary restrictions that we may add through our reasoning. The latter are subject to conditions of time and place, and are amended according to experience. We may legislate some restriction and in time we realize that it does not meet what is required, or that it is excessive, and we then amend it.

It may happen that some special circumstances make a particular matter, which is permissible or recommended or obligatory, a cause of temptation that needs to be prevented. Temptation can be general with effects engulfing the whole community, or particular to an individual or a group of individuals. When temptation is general, then society should deal with it through its leadership of scholars and people of authority. Temptation faced by individuals are considered by those who experience it or the people of the area where it occurs, or a scholar who is asked about it. In all these situations, temporary temptation which restricts what is permissible should be judged as it is, in the same way as necessity which permits what is forbidden is estimated and considered.

The imposition of unnecessary restrictions under the pretext of cause prevention is an act of evasion by people who do not want to face life. Some people have resorted to extremism in their worship, preferring a life of seclusion, so that they do not face temptation. They would have done better to face life's temptations with strong resolve and adherence to Islamic values and standards. Likewise, those who impose stringent restrictions resort to similar evasion. They, or their women folk, turn away from facing life and participating in its various fields. By doing so, they deprive Islamic society of much good. What Islam requires of everyone is adherence to its principles and values with fair resolve. They will then be able to implement God's code of law with whatever it permits, recommends and makes obligatory, as also what it discourages or forbids. This allows the character of the Muslim woman to develop. She can then be productive and creative, within the family or in appropriate social activities.

The proper course of action for all Muslims and Muslim societies is to implement the Prophet's Sunnah with its moderate restrictions that reflect a set of fine manners. We may then add some precautionary measures in the light of what experience presents. Is this not better than to organize our social life on the basis of exaggerated restrictions and unnecessary precautions? In our present time, some of us continue to resort to extremism in the application of the rule of cause prevention in the area of sexual temptation. This leads to the restriction of many permissible things, wrongly changing their status into discouragement or prohibition. As mentioned earlier, what is needed is to protect permissible matters against extreme strictness that gives them a foul status while the Shariah classifies them as good. God's Messenger (peace be upon him) said: 'Every king has a sanctuary, and truly God's sanctuary on earth is His prohibitions.'[13] (Related by al-Bukhari and Muslim) It is clear transgression to trespass on God's sanctuary, while it is wise not to draw too close to it. By the same token, it is stupid and foolish not to enjoy the broad area that God has made permissible. A person who commits what is forbidden wrongs himself, but the one who forbids himself and others what God has permitted wrongs himself and other people.

In this area, two attitudes are wrong. The first is that of a person who disdains to do a number of permissible things in the area of social mixing between men and women. Thus, he rejects that women should pray in mosques; that they should listen to the lectures of a male scholar, whether in general meetings or in 'female-only' circles; that greetings are exchanged between men and women; that men and women should enjoin each other to do what is right and avoid what is wrong, and that women may drive. As such, a man disdains doing any of these, he does not say whether they are forbidden or discouraged. He merely and disdainfully refrains from them at all times. This attitude is wrong on two counts: the first is to disdain doing what is permissible. We have shown that God's Messenger (peace be upon him) censured such an attitude when some of his Companions tended towards this. The other is that it leaves oneself and one's immediate circle confused, because what is permissible becomes confused with what is discouraged and prohibited. When disdaining to do the permissible continues for some time, it gives the impression that it is polluted with what is unbecoming of a believer. Thus, the purity of the permissible, which is stated by the Shariah, is negated and one of God's rulings is discarded. We have already mentioned that scholars of legal theory make clear that rulings must be kept clear, with no confusion.

---

13. 'His prohibitions' means doing what God has pronounced as forbidden or refraining from doing what He has commanded. Both incur a sin. – Author's note.

The second attitude is that of a person who, in his desire to ensure safety from temptation, uses the rule of cause prevention to pronounce a set of permissible matters as discouraged or forbidden, without explaining that these matters are permissible in the first place but where their discouragement or prohibition results from certain temporary circumstances. When such circumstances do not apply, these matters revert to their original ruling of permissibility. The problem with this attitude is that it leaves people confused about what God has ruled concerning some matters. Hence, they think that something is forbidden or discouraged when it is in fact permitted by God. On the other hand, since the verdict of discouragement or prohibition is based on the rule of cause prevention, then it is a view arrived at through reasoning. It does not rely on any text in God's Book or the Prophet's Sunnah. Therefore, whoever upholds this ruling should be careful, because it is merely the personal view of whoever has advanced it. Anyone's view may be right or wrong. Hence, the one who expresses this view, stating it to others, must make it clear that it is based on personal reasoning, admitting the possibility of error. It must never be represented as a categorical ruling given by God, the Exalted.

Here are some cases that merit reflection. Ibn al-Qayyim says in his book, *I'lām al-Muwaqqi'īn*:

> The Prophet's Companions used their reasoning and arrived at certain conclusions. However, none of them considered that his conclusion was God's ruling. He would say: 'This is my view: if it is correct, then this is by God's grace, and if it is wrong, the error is mine. God and His Messenger are free from my error.' This is reported from several scholars among the Prophet's Companions, including Abu Bakr, 'Umar and Ibn Mas'ūd. Moreover, they did not require anyone else to uphold their views. Everyone can have their own views on the basis of their reasoning. This

> is reflected in the example of 'Umar ibn al-Khaṭṭāb when he met a man and asked him: 'What have you done?' He said: ''Alī and Zayd gave me such-and-such ruling.' 'Umar said: 'I would have given a different judgement.' The man said: 'What prevents you, when you are in the position of authority?' He said: 'Had I been giving a ruling on the basis of God's Book and the Prophet's Sunnah, I would have done that. I am merely giving an opinion, and everyone is entitled to their opinion.' Thus, 'Umar did not invalidate the judgement given by 'Alī and Zayd.

Ibn al-Qayyim also said: 'God, the Exalted, has also forbidden that anyone should say of anything God has not stated to be forbidden, "this is permissible and that is forbidden." He describes the one who says this as a fabricator of falsehood. He says: "Do not say – for any false thing you may utter with your tongues – that 'This is lawful and this is forbidden', so as to attribute your lying inventions to God."' (16: 116)

In his book *Jāmi' Bayān al-'Ilm wa Faḍlih*, Ibn 'Abd al-Barr says:

> Rabī'ah ibn Abi 'Abd al-Raḥmān said to Ibn Shihāb: 'When you, Abu Bakr, explain your view to people, tell them that it is your own view. When you tell them something from the Sunnah, tell them that it is the Sunnah.'

> Mālik ibn Anas said: 'It was not the practice of people, or anyone in past generations, to say about anything: "This is permissible and this is forbidden." Nor did I meet anyone whose example I follow who says the same. None dared say this. They would only say: "We dislike this, and we think this is fine." "We steer away from this, and we do not approve of that." They never said: "This is permissible and that is forbidden." Have you not heard what God, Mighty

> and Exalted, said: Say: "Do but consider all the means of sustenance that God has bestowed on you! Some of it you then made unlawful, and some lawful." Say: 'Has God given you leave to do so, or do you fabricate lies against God?' (10: 59) The permissible is what is permitted by God and His Messenger, and the forbidden is what God and His Messenger prohibited.'"
>
> What Mālik meant is that whatever we arrive at through reasoning, preferring it to other alternatives, we should not describe as permissible or forbidden, but God knows best.

To our brothers who are keen to protect the honour of all Muslims, we say: Issuing a ruling of total prohibition through the rule of cause prevention often remains short of understanding all circumstances attached to the prohibited thing, and recognizing what it produces of benefit. It also falls short of understanding the circumstances of all people and appreciating that they have different moral standards. When God, the Legislator, states something as permissible, letting people choose to do it or leave it, He takes into consideration that people have different circumstances and interests, as also different standards of morality and psychological conditions.

Taking an extreme attitude has led hard liners to deviate from the guidance of God, the Wise who knows all. His guidance prefers the gentle and easy approach. It made them invent several layers of restriction and impose layers of pressure. In doing so, they have limited women's movement and activity, whether permissible, recommended or a duty. They, thus, imposed on both man and woman various forms of difficulty and hardship for which God has given no sanction. Compassionate to all His servants, God, the Ever-Merciful, says: 'God desires that you have ease. He does not desire that you be afflicted with hardship.' (2: 185) God's Messenger (peace be upon him) says: 'Beware of resorting to extremism in religion. Communities before you were ruined by extremism in religion.' 'Ā'ishah reports about the Prophet: 'Whenever God's Messenger had a choice between two alternatives, he would choose the easier option, unless it be sinful.' (Related by al-Bukhari and Muslim) Our scholars have deduced the rule that says, 'Hardship calls for relaxation', on the basis of the Qur'an and the Prophet's Sunnah. This rule means that when something which is required by religion involves hardship, then the rules pertaining to it should be relaxed allowing the one who faces such hardship to overlook some aspects of the duty in order to relieve the hardship. Faced with all this emphasis on ease in our compassionate Shariah, why do we restrict much of what our faith has made easy?

There is a great difference between preventing a meeting between men and women at a particular time, or in a particular situation, in order to ensure safety from an occasional temptation, while allowing such meeting in general situations and preventing all meetings between men and women in all situations under the pretext of such safety from temptation. The first is a proper measure because it maintains the original permissibility. Indeed, it adheres to the Sunnah, as the prevention occurs in a particular situation that calls for the application of the rule of cause prevention. The second case is wrong and Islamically unacceptable, because it totally negates a permissible measure. In other words, we pronounced it as forbidden, as though we abrogate the Legislator's ruling of permissibility.

The question to be asked is: have the measures that disallow uncovering women's faces and depriving them of participation in social life led to the total prevention of immorality? We think that they have not. Indeed, they could not, considering that they are contrary to the Prophet's guidance. Tricks will be used so that people can enjoy their forbidden pleasure. Were we to raise iron barriers between men and women, those who are driven by desire, eager to satisfy it in any way would have tried hard to find some weak points in such barriers. In most cases, such weak points are found and infiltration takes place. But if the barriers are too strong for them, men and women would still try to have their pleasure, resorting to homosexuality or lesbianism. In the past, people used to circulate jokes centred around sex, and then they had their pornographic magazines. Later, pornographic films and videos of all types became easy to access. Nowadays, social media plays a major role in spreading all this. Thus, strict regulations could not stamp out immoral behaviour, as different measures of it are intrinsic in human society. Indeed, pursuing an extreme hard line leads to increased immorality.

In conclusion, we give the following comments by a twentieth century scholar about a hadith we mentioned earlier. ''Abdullāh ibn 'Umar said: "I heard God's Messenger say: 'Do not stop your women from attending mosques when they ask permission to go there.' Bilāl ibn 'Abdullāh said: "By God, we will stop them, so that they do not use that as a cover for something untoward." His father went up to him, hurling on him such strong verbal abuse as I never heard him use before. He said to him: "I narrate something from God's Messenger (peace be upon him) and you still say, 'we will stop them?.''' (Related by Muslim)

'Abd al-Ḥamīd ibn Bādīs said: 'Ignorant and deviant people often say something similar to what Bilāl said, because they always embraced deviation, so that to them it became a sunnah, while they consider the Prophet's Sunnah to constitute deviation. When you mention the proper Islamic ruling, and the Qur'anic or hadith evidence on which it is based, they turn away and refuse to obey. They either declare their opposition, or resort to silence while intending to still disobey. This is not the way good believers follow. Whenever a Muslim hears a religious ruling and a Qur'anic text or a hadith in support, he must willingly embrace it. It is imperative that a Muslim does not take an opposite attitude. We must never feel unhappy with a ruling given by God and His Messenger. On the contrary, we must welcome it with trust.'

Factors Leading to Extremism in the Application of the Rule of Cause Prevention

The factors leading to extremism require an in-depth study based on careful and detailed analysis that relies on a comprehensive view that takes all aspects of this phenomenon into account. We will highlight a number of possible factors, making no claim that what we mention covers all factors. God alone knows what people may think or feel. What we assert is that there is a tendency towards extremism in the application of the rule of cause prevention. This is reflected in the disregard of the principles laid down by scholars of legal theory for the application of this rule. A tendency to be so extreme has also been shown by some eminent scholars. We appreciate their knowledge and scholarship, but we say: Blessed is the One who never errs.

Factor 1: Unawareness of the conditions applicable to the rule of cause prevention

We cited earlier what scholars said about the rule of cause prevention. They clearly show that there are several conditions that must be observed when disallowing any permissible thing as a cause of harm or a foul result. These conditions are:

1. That the permissible thing leads to harm in most cases, not rarely. Al-Shāṭibī adds that when it often leads to harm, but neither in the majority of cases nor rarely, it may not be disallowed, because in this situation, either one of the two outcomes may occur, with nothing to suggest that either is more likely.
2. That the foul result is greater than the benefit, i.e. it is not merely a lesser outcome.
3. When the above two conditions are met, no ruling of total prohibition is acceptable. The ruling ranges between discouragement and prohibition according to the extent of the resulting harm.
4. If the deed leads to some foul result, but its benefit is greater than the foul result, the Shariah does not merely permit it, it may consider it desirable or a duty, according to the extent of the benefit.

Although these statements of scholars of legal theory are very clear, some later scholars have been unaware of them, and this led to extremism in the application of the rule with regard to preventing the causes of temptation as regards women.

Factor 2: Misunderstanding of the meaning of women's temptation

Hadith texts make it clear that God, the Wise Legislator, has not cut off every link between man and woman. On the contrary, He wants there to be bridges for cooperation between them in building sound human life on earth. In order for these bridges to remain operative, Islam allows men to see the best of a woman, i.e. her face, including the prettiest of women.[14] A young believer looks at her, lowers his gaze and remains patient. He may resort to fasting to weaken his desire, if he cannot afford to get married. An adult believer sees her, lowers his gaze and remains patient. He then resolves to get married and begins to prepare for that. A married believer sees her, lowers his gaze and goes to his wife to satisfy his desire. A weak believer sees her and keeps looking at her. He may also commit some minor offence. A transgressor sees her and stares hard. He may commit a grave offence. However, neither the minor nor the grave offences are due to the woman uncovering her face. They are due to those men. The weak one may give way to his weakness, even without seeing a woman's face, and may still commit the minor offence. The transgressor may give way to his desire and resort to various methods to penetrate through the barriers erected by extremists.

Reinforcing these bridges, Islamic law gives women ample scope to participate in social life and to meet men in serious and proper situations, so that life continues with ease and comfort. Had God wanted that such bridges do not exist and wanted to enforce total separation between men and women, He would have given a clear and decisive command to women to cover their faces. He would not have

14. When we say 'including the prettiest of women', this is not something we say at our own behest. We use it because it is used in several religious texts, such as: (1) the Qur'anic verse that says to the Prophet: 'You [Muhammad] are not permitted to take any further wives, nor to exchange these for other wives, even though you are attracted by their beauty' (33: 52) (2); The woman from Khath'am who stopped to request the Prophet's ruling is described in the hadith as 'pretty', and (3) Many hadiths mention that the female Companions of the Prophet used to keep their faces uncovered during his lifetime. There is no doubt that some of them were very pretty. Indeed, at times, this is clearly mentioned. (See, Chapter 3 of Volume 4 of this series) – Author's note.

given a clear order to men to lower their gaze, for what would they be gazing at? A black ghost? This is not something that we imagine to come from God, the Wise who knows all. Had the Legislator wanted women not to participate in social life, the Prophet would not have ordered men not to stop their women from going to mosques, and he would not have ordered all women to attend the Eid Prayer. He would not have allowed women to join the army in order to take care of the wounded and give water to thirsty fighters. He would not have allowed a man to visit a woman whose husband was away, provided that he was accompanied by one or two other men.

Therefore, every Muslim should realize that, aware of the natural tendency of men and women to incline towards each other, the Wise Legislator took the appropriate measures to prevent temptation, ordering both men and women to lower their gaze at each other. Moreover, God highlighted certain manners to be observed when men and women meet. Whoever finds himself too weak to observe this way of treatment can blame only himself. He should work hard to overcome his weakness. If he finds lowering his gaze too hard, he should know that this is a hardship God has set as a test for all men and women.

The measures taken by Islam work well to reduce the temptation to the lowest possible level. In saying so, we rely on the practical implementation of these measures during the Prophet's lifetime. In addition, we have another, centuries old implementation that has been approved of by scholars. We see it in rural areas in Egypt, Syria, Palestine and other Muslim countries. There is close similarity between this implementation and its counterpart in the Prophet's lifetime. It allows women to participate in all aspects of social life and to meet men whenever such meeting is needed, always adhering to the standards of propriety applicable to both men and women.

There are, thus, two levels of temptation. The first is that of a transitory feeling that occurs to a Muslim. He may lower his gaze, seek God's shelter and attend to his business, or stare fixedly, entertain some thoughts or indulge in some minor sin, then turn to God in repentance. A third possibility is that he continues neglecting his duty. Such sins are normally forgiven by God's grace. He says: 'He will reward those who do good with what is best. As for those who avoid grave sins and shameful deeds, apart from casual indulgence, your Lord is abounding in forgiveness.' (53: 31–32)

Ibn 'Abbās said: 'I do not know anything akin to casual indulgence than what Abu Hurayrah has narrated from the Prophet (peace be upon him): "God has assigned to every human being his share of fornication, and everyone shall inevitably have that. The eye fornicates by looking; the tongue fornicates by speech; and one desires and hopes. The genital organ will either confirm all this or steer away."' (Related by al-Bukhari and Muslim)

We mentioned earlier what ensures the forgiveness of minor sins. The Prophet says: 'When a Muslim or a believer servant of God performs the ablution and washes his face, he is freed from every sin he looked at, as the sin departs from him along with the water, or with the last drop of water.' (Related by Muslim) He also says: 'The five daily prayers, the Friday Prayer to the next Friday Prayer, and Ramadan to Ramadan are ways to erase sins committed between them, as long as the major sins are avoided.' (Related by Muslim)

This level of temptation may occur to a Muslim even though he lives in the purest of societies, like the one the Prophet established in Madinah. When we discussed the Prophet's guidance on the implementation of the rule of cause prevention, we noted that his Companions were troubled by such temptation to the point that they sought his permission to emasculate themselves. Indeed, this level of temptation may occur to a person when he is totally cut off from all women. Some images may cross his mind, or some thoughts may occur to him. This is due to the fact that God has placed in human nature a strong attraction to the opposite sex. Needless to say, the attraction will be stronger when we live in normal human society. Moreover, promptings from Satan occur to every Muslim in respect of every type of desire, such as love of money, children, status, leadership, and indeed sex. A Muslim strives hard, all the time to steer away from what is forbidden in the satisfaction of all these desires. Such striving enhances his personality and strengthens his willpower. Moreover, it gives him a healthy mentality. This level of temptation is expected when men and women meet, as God has allowed. It occurred during the Prophet's lifetime, as mentioned earlier.

The other level of temptation is the very strong one that leads to fornication or adultery. It is very unlikely to happen in normal meetings between men and women. Yet, it may happen on very rare occasions, but such a rare event is not given a ruling. As we mentioned earlier, it occurred during the Prophet's lifetime, but the Prophet did not order women to cover their faces or to stop meeting men as a result. Therefore, if we set aside all wrong ideas that result from the misunderstanding of the meaning of temptation and try to understand the nature of the temptation to guard against, we realize that it occurs, in the majority of cases, when people disregard the Islamic manners God wants Muslims to observe. Since God, who knows well the woman's attraction and temptation, has established these manners, He certainly knows that they are sufficient to ensure safety from temptation. He is the One who knows all. What we are referring to here is the strong temptation that leads to the cardinal sin of adultery, with its preliminaries and far-reaching results including the destruction of families and family life.

People may say that casual temptation may lead to stronger and longer lasting temptation. This is true, but rare. As we noted, scholars of legal theory state that a permissible matter may be disallowed on the basis of cause prevention if it leads to foul results in the majority of cases, not rarely. We have discussed this in detail. Therefore, and in order that we do not alter God's law as suits us, we need to point out a very important thing: temptation that requires disallowing or prohibiting what is permissible must meet certain standards. We can identify these standards from the Prophet's Sunnah and also from what leading scholars have established. Here are the most important of these standards.

1. The temptation is not merely one man or several men staring at a woman. The evidence for this is the hadith narrated by Ibn 'Abbās: 'Al-Faḍl ('Abdullāh's brother) was riding behind the Prophet when a woman from Khath'am spoke to the Prophet. Al-Faḍl kept gazing at her and she looked at him. The Prophet kept turning al-Faḍl's face to the other direction....' (Related by al-Bukhari and Muslim) If this was done by al-Faḍl when he was sharing the same mount with the Prophet, it is more likely to be done by others. Yet the Prophet did not order the woman to cover her face, or to stay away from places where men are around. He merely diverted al-Faḍl's gaze.
2. The temptation is not merely some irritating words some men may direct at a woman. The evidence for this is the Qur'anic verse that says: 'Prophet! Say to your wives, daughters and all believing women that they should draw over themselves some of their outer garments. This will be more conducive to their being recognized and not affronted.' (33: 59) Commenting on this verse, al-Ṭabarī says: 'God, the Exalted, orders His Prophet to tell his wives, daughters and all believing women that they must not go about wearing clothes similar to what slave women wear. They should draw some of their outer garments over themselves. Thus, everyone will know that they are free women and no transgressor will affront them with foul words.'

This refers to the presence of hypocrites and weak-minded people in Madinah, and some bedouins coming from desert areas without having been properly educated by the Prophet. Impolite behaviour that may exceed staring hard or using foul words was expected from such people. Nevertheless, the Prophet did not order Muslim women to cover their faces, nor did he place a barrier separating the women's area in the mosque. He did not restrict women going out to attend to their needs. The examples of women's participation in social life and their meetings with men in all areas of life prove this. Chapter 4 of Volume 2 of this series includes many such examples.

3. It must not be the result of a particular event, or an individual case. There were some individual cases of this type, but the Prophet did not react by issuing an order of prohibition to ensure safety from temptation. We mentioned such cases earlier.

God, the All-Knowing, certainly knows the general human weakness, and He, in His infinite wisdom, takes care of it through a set of fine manners that cause no problem to any man or woman and do not disrupt life activity. We must differentiate between this general human weakness and the wrong idea that leads some people to misunderstand the meaning of the temptation that God ordered us to steer away from and to prevent its causes. These people imagine that temptation occurs merely by the presence of a woman, even though she observes all required Islamic manners. They imagine the temptation to occur with every movement a woman takes, even though it be no more than taking a few steps, and every sound she makes, even if she says a few serious words, and whatever appears of her body, even if it is only her face or finger. Their imagination again overpowers them making them think that gross indecency may occur at every moment. They, thus, fear that a scandal may burst out at every moment. Such imaginary fears are often supported by unauthentic reports or by wrong explanations of authentic texts. As a result, many Muslims have come to believe that the primary view of the Shariah is that women stay away from men's places and meetings, coming in contact with them only in cases of necessity or urgent need. This understanding has lingered for many centuries, so that it is taken for granted.

The truth is that highly authentic texts provide, in total, definitive evidence proving that women's attendance with men, observing Islamic manners, is deemed free of temptation which is outlawed and warned against by Islam. It is the basic norm that women participate in serious life affairs. These are often frequented by men, but such is human life: sometimes men are present and sometimes they are not. Women participate in life affairs whether men are present or absent. In other words, women should not be too worried about the presence of men: their presence should neither encourage nor stop women's attendance. Likewise, men should not be bothered about women's presence. Their presence should neither encourage nor stop men participating. If such meetings involve a measure of fleeting temptation, this is perfectly natural, and God makes this one aspect of the test of life to which men and women are subjected.

We finally draw the attention of our brethren who are highly protective of Muslims' honour to the fact that too much avoidance of meeting between men and women leads to a misconception of what constitutes temptation. In other words, it leads to imagining temptation where none exists. It also leads to worry about temptation shortly before such a meeting, and feeling its exaggerated pressure during the meeting. On the other hand, a moderate approach that allows such mixed meetings, with the observance of Islamic manners, leads to a correct and balanced understanding of temptation. It also leads to a balanced approach towards it, its expectation and its experience.

Factor 3: Thinking ill of the woman and keeping her weak

Prior to Islam, women suffered various forms of contemptuous and humiliating treatment. Islam took care to remove women's burdens and shackles. This is confirmed by the following texts:

Umm Salamah narrated: 'A woman came to God's Messenger (peace be upon him) and said that her daughter's husband had died... The Prophet said to her: "... Yet, in pre-Islamic days, none of you could finish her mourning before the turn of a year." Zaynab bint Abu Salamah explained the meaning of the hadith and said: 'When a woman lost her husband in pre-Islamic days, she would sit in a small tent of hair, wearing her worst clothes, and touching no perfume for a whole year. She would then be brought an animal, such as an ass or sheep or bird, to rub her skin on it. In most cases such an animal died soon afterwards. She was then given a piece of camel dropping to throw away. She could then wear perfume and do normal things.' (Related by al-Bukhari and Muslim)

'Umar ibn al-Khaṭṭāb narrated: 'In pre-Islamic days we cared nothing for women. Then God revealed whatever He did concerning them and assigned to them their rights. 'Umar said: 'Once I was deliberating within myself about a particular matter when my wife said, "It may be appropriate if you do such-and-such."' I said, And why do you interfere in something of my concerns? She said, "This is amazing coming from you, Ibn al-Khaṭṭāb! You object to being spoken to, when your daughter[15] argues with God's Messenger (peace be upon him) and he may remain angry for the rest of the day!"' (Related by al-Bukhari and Muslim) Another version quotes 'Umar: 'In pre-Islamic days we cared nothing for women. With the advent of Islam, God mentioned them and we felt that we owe them a duty, but we did not involve them in our affairs.'

15. His daughter was Hafsah, the Prophet's wife.

Al-Ṭabarānī quotes ‘Umar: ‘When we were in Makkah, we did not talk to our wives. A wife was a servant at home. When a husband needed her, he would pull her by her legs and get his satisfaction. When we moved to Madinah, our women learnt from the women of the Anṣār, and they would argue with us.’

Iyās ibn ‘Abdullāh said: ‘God’s Messenger (peace be upon him) said: “Do not beat God’s female servants.” ‘Umar later came to the Prophet and said: “Women have become undisciplined.” The Prophet gave a concession allowing men to hit them.[16] Many women visited the Prophet’s family complaining about their husbands. The Prophet said: “Many women visited Muhammad’s family complaining about their husbands. Those are not your good men.”’ (Related by Abu Dāwūd)

Islam has elevated the status of women, treating them as those sharing with men the honour God has given them as He says: ‘We have indeed honoured the children of Adam.’ (17: 70) Women share with men the same human status and bear the same responsibility for crime. God says: ‘Their Lord answers them: “I will not suffer the work of any worker among you, male or female, to be lost. Each of you is an issue of the other.”’ (3: 195) ‘As for the man or the woman who is guilty of stealing, cut off their hands.’ (5: 38) ‘As for the adulteress and the adulterer, flog each of them with a hundred stripes.’ (24: 2) When Islam gave the woman this status, some beautiful examples emerged showing a woman’s strong character and good awareness of her responsibilities. Here are some examples:

- ‘Ātikah bint Zayd used to attend the congregational prayer in the mosque, benefiting by the status given to women by the Prophet. Ibn ‘Umar narrated: ‘One of ‘Umar’s wives regularly

16. It appears that the Prophet intended this as a temporary measure to show in practice that such a measure will never produce a proper family atmosphere.

attended the Fajr and 'Isha prayers with the congregation at the mosque. She was asked: "Why do you come out for these prayers when you know that 'Umar dislikes this and is jealous?" She said: "Why does he not stop me?" They said: "He is prevented by the Prophet's order: 'Do not stop women servants of God from attending God's mosques.'"" (Related by al-Bukhari)

- Independently from her husband, Hind bint 'Utbah greets the Prophet: 'Ā'ishah narrated that Hind bint 'Utbah said: 'Messenger of God, there was a time when no people on the face of the earth I loved to be more humbled than your own family, but today there are no people on the face of the earth I love to be more honoured than your own family.' He said: 'And I, too. By Him who holds my soul in His hand.' (Related by al-Bukhari and Muslim)
- Umm Ḥarām requests the Prophet to pray that she joins the first maritime expedition: Anas ibn Mālik reports: 'The Prophet used to visit Umm Ḥarām bint Milḥān... He once slept (at her place) and when he woke up, he smiled. She asked him what caused him to smile. He said: "I was shown a group of my followers going out for jihad, riding into the sea, looking like kings on their thrones...." She said: 'Messenger of God! Pray to God to make me one of them.' He prayed for her as she requested.' (Related by al-Bukhari and Muslim)

Despite the emergence of such examples during the Prophet's lifetime, a long time was needed, as well as constant reminders and serious implementation, before age-old concepts and habits could be totally discarded, so as to allow Islamic values to properly settle among the Arabs. Old ideas continued to linger on, such as Bilāl ibn 'Abdullāh's attitude towards the women's attending 'Ishā Prayer in the mosque. He said that they would use it as a cover up for something untoward. When Islam spread far and wide within a very short period, many communities adopted it, bringing with them some of their old traditions and misconceptions. This led to increased deviation from God's guidance. This is highlighted by Ibn Taymiyyah: 'The Shariah orders that Muslims should not emulate the non-Arabs… This includes those non-Arab Muslims whose behaviour differs from that of early Muslims. Likewise, Arabian ignorance refers to what the Arabs used to do in the days of ignorance before the advent of Islam, and the practices of the old days of ignorance to which many Arabs later reverted.' We will not give a detailed discussion of the influence of old ignorant practices, by Arabs and non-Arabs, on the Muslim mind. We hope that this topic will be studied in depth, but our task here is to show the divine guidance as reflected in the text of the Qur'an and the Prophet's hadiths.

With the passage of several centuries, God's guidance in respect of the status of women was increasingly ignored with the result that men came to look at women as humans with a lowly status. They thought her either a weak-minded person deceived by foolish words, or a wicked schemer up to no good. In either case, she was not perceived as a full and mature human being. Rather, she was only there for sexual play. This is even stated in some poetry. As such, there was no need for her to attend the congregational night worship in the mosque during Ramadan. She needed only to fulfil the minimum of worship requirements. She did not need to attend scholars' circles in mosques, because the minimum of religious knowledge was sufficient for her! Indeed, her education came to be totally neglected. She need not share her husband's worries, or accompany him on his travels. The minimum amount of care was sufficient for her. She need not share in any social activity, as the minimum amount of reward was enough for her. Such illogical attitudes covered all aspects of the woman's life. It is enough to look at a hadith anthology dating back to the end of the second century of the Islamic calendar, such as *al-Muṣannaf* by Ibn Abi Shaybah, to find examples of such extreme views. Ibn Abi Shaybah, in fact, lists the texts showing the correct, balanced view, but the fact that he also enters the other type shows how false claims that are contrary to the divine faith penetrated into the Muslim consciousness. Here are some examples:

- It is not permissible for a man to perform the ablution using the excess water remaining after a woman had performed her ablution;
- A man may not drink the water in a cup used by a woman during her menstruation;
- A wife may not have a bath using the water from the same container as her husband;
- A woman may not lead a congregational prayer of women;
- A woman may not attend congregational or Friday prayers;
- A woman may not attend the Eid Prayer, and
- A woman may not repeat the phrases of God's glorification, i.e. *takbīr*, on Eid days.

When men think so ill of women generally, they also tend to treat them with high-handedness. The woman's appeal is one of the temptations with which God tests people in this present life. Why does extremism in the application of the rule of cause prevention concentrate only on female temptation? Why do the extremists impose such restrictions on women thinking that they are, thus, safe from female temptation? The extensive application of this rule of cause prevention has continued for many centuries, but when we study it, we wonder why this extensive application focuses only on women's temptation and not on other forms of temptation? The extremists often argue that times have changed and moral corruption has spread. In fact, moral corruption leads to the weakness of resistance to all forms of temptation, not merely the sexual aspect.

God's Messenger (peace be upon him) has certainly warned us against the temptation presented by women. Here are two of the many hadiths stating such warnings. Usāmah ibn Zayd narrated that the Prophet (peace be upon him) said: 'I do not leave behind a worse temptation for men than women.' (Related by al-Bukhari and Muslim) Abu Sa'īd al-Khudrī quotes the Prophet (peace be upon him) saying: 'Beware of (the temptation of) women. The first deviation by the Children of Israel was through (the temptation of) women.' (Related by Muslim)

However, we also have many hadith texts in which the Prophet (peace be upon him) warns against the temptation of wealth. Here are a few:

- Abu Sa'īd al-Khudrī said that God's Messenger (peace be upon him) said: 'What I fear most for you is what God brings forth for you of the earth's blessings. People asked: 'What are the blessings of the earth?' He said: 'The splendour of the life of this world.' (Related by al-Bukhari)
- 'Amr ibn 'Awf narrated that the Prophet (peace be upon him) said: 'By God, I do not fear poverty for you. What I fear for you is that worldly comforts are given to you in plenty, as they were given to communities before you. You will then compete for these as they competed, and they will distract you as they were distracted.' (Related by al-Bukhari)
- Ka'b ibn 'Iyāḍ said: 'I heard God's Messenger say: 'Each community is tested by a temptation, and the temptation for my community is wealth.' (Related by al-Tirmidhī)
- Abu al-Dardā' narrated from the Prophet (peace be upon him): 'By Him who holds my soul in His hand, worldly comforts will be given to you in plenty, so that it will be the only thing that causes the heart of any one of you to swerve from the truth.' (Related by Ibn Mājah)

God and His Messenger also warn us against the temptation presented by one's offspring. This has several manifestations, including:

1. Favouring some of one's children with extra love. This is what happened in the case of Prophet Joseph whose brothers

thought that their father loved the child Joseph and his younger brother more than he loved them. God said: 'They said (to one another]: Truly, Joseph and his brother are dearer to our father than we, even though we are many. Surely our father is in manifest error. Kill Joseph, or cast him away in some faraway land, so that you have your father's attention turned to you alone. After that you will (Repent and) be righteous people.' (12: 8-9)

2. Favouring a child with a gift, as happened to some of the Prophet's Companions. Al-Nuʿmān ibn Bashīr narrated: 'My mother asked my father to give me some gift. He subsequently thought about it and gave me a gift. She said to him: "I am not satisfied until you have asked the Prophet to witness it." He took me, when I was a young lad, going to the Prophet (peace be upon him). He said to him: "This child's mother, bint Rawāḥah, has asked me to give this child of mine some gift." The Prophet asked him: "Do you have other children?" He said: "Yes." (Another version of the hadith mentions that the Prophet asked him: "Have you given all your other children a similar gift?" He said: "No") God's Messenger (peace be upon him) said: "Do not ask me to witness injustice."' (Related by al-Bukhari and Muslim)
3. Abstaining from jihad, whether verbal or in war, in fear for them. Al-Aswad ibn Khalaf mentioned that God's Messenger (peace be upon him) said: 'Children cause a person to be miserly, coward, ignorant and sorrowful.' (Related by al-Ḥākim)

In His infinite wisdom, God, the Legislator, has set a number of manners and controls to deal with the temptations of wealth and children, in the same way as He did with the temptation of women, with regard to the uncovering of their faces and meeting with men. These manners and controls include:

- Giving a general warning against the temptation of money and children. God says: 'Know that your worldly goods and children are but a trial.' (8: 28)
- The prohibition of favouring some children above others. God's Messenger (peace be upon him) said: 'Fear God and maintain fairness between your children.' (Related by al-Bukhari and Muslim)
- The prohibition of stinginess. God says: 'To those who hoard up gold and silver and do not spend them in God's cause, give the news of a painful suffering.' (9: 34) The Prophet (peace be upon him) said: 'Beware of stinginess; it brought ruin to communities before your time.' (Related by Muslim)
- The prohibition of staying away from jihad because of one's love of one's children and property. God says: 'Say: If your fathers, your sons, your brothers, your spouses, your clan, and the property you have acquired, and the business in which you fear a decline, and the dwellings in which you take pleasure, are dearer to you than God and His Messenger and the struggle in His cause, then wait until God shall make manifest His will. God does not provide guidance to the transgressors.' (9: 24)
- The prohibition of taking money unlawfully. God says: 'Believers, do not gorge yourselves on usury, doubling your money again and again.' (3: 130) 'Those who devour the property of orphans unjustly, only swallow fire into their bellies. They will be made to endure a blazing fire.' (4: 10) 'Do not devour one another's property wrongfully, nor bribe with it the judges in order that you may sinfully, and knowingly, deprive others of any part of what is rightfully theirs.' (2: 188)

In Muslim society, men live with their children and they conduct their transactions with money. They are always subject to the temptations of worldly comforts and children. Some fear God and spare themselves such temptations, while others disobey God and succumb to these temptations in different degrees. No one advocated the prohibition of marrying more than one wife so that the man would not favour the children of one of his wives over those of another. Nor did anyone advocate celibacy or staying childless so that he would not be driven by the love of his children to be tight-fisted or cowardly, unwilling to donate for good causes or fight for God's cause. Apart from a few Sufis, no one advocated countering the temptation of wealth by refusing to own more than what is enough to meet one's essential needs.

Why is it, then, that we do not see any exaggeration in the application of the rule of cause prevention to counter the temptations of wealth and children, in the same way as the exaggeration in its application to female temptation? Yet God warns against all three temptations in the same verse of the Qur'an. He says: 'Alluring to man is the enjoyment of worldly desires through women and offspring, heaped-up treasures of gold and silver, horses of high mark, cattle and plantations. These are the comforts of this life. With God is the best of all goals.' (3: 14)

It may be said that female temptation is the strongest, as God's Messenger (peace be upon him) said: 'I do not leave behind a worse temptation for men than women.' (Related by al-Bukhari and Muslim) This is certainly true, but it is also true that God's Messenger, who was well aware of the strength of this temptation, has shown us the proper way to safeguard against it. Why, then, should we add to what the Legislator, in His infinite wisdom, has set for us? We believe that it is due to a particular factor that is added to what we have mentioned and will be presently mentioning. This factor is male dominance over females, and the arrogance with which men treat women. The burden of every aspect of the hard-line stance taken in respect of female temptation is shouldered by the woman, not the man. By contrast, taking a hard-line approach in respect of the temptation presented by money and children requires men to show strong resolve, and its burden is shouldered by men. Moreover, the woman cannot repel, or even object to the hardship placed on her as a result. She is powerless, like a captive person or a slave facing his master. In fact, men have been unfair to women while women have had no support. Men have favoured themselves and there was none to hold them to account.

Let us look at the measures the extremists took to counter the female temptation, so as to realize how much hardship has been placed on women, depriving them of much that is good, while men have remained totally safe. They forced women to always cover their faces, thus restricting God's gift of eyesight and her need to breathe clean air. They stopped her from going to mosque, depriving her of listening to the Qur'an and scholars' admonition, receiving religious education and meeting other Muslim women. They stopped her from attending the Eid Prayer, depriving her of participating in God's praise and glorification as well as witnessing the goodness of the occasion and the believers' function. They prevented her from investing her money, requiring her to assign this to one of her close relatives. This denies her one of her own rights and presents the risk of loss of all or some of her money through whoever is appointed as her agent. They stopped her from working to earn her living when she needs this, forcing her to remain dependent on others. They, thus, deprive her of the right to dignified life. What is most strange is that in all these aspects, they take a line that is directly opposite to what was the practice during the Prophet's lifetime.

Let us consider the attitude of some of the Prophet's Companions when they wanted to prevent women's temptation and feared suffering hardship. They thought of taking an extreme measure to resist the temptation, requesting permission to emasculate themselves. Abu Hurayrah reports that he said: 'Messenger of God, I am a young man and I fear that I find things hard. I cannot afford to get married. The Prophet gave me no answer. I later said the same and he gave me no answer. I again said the same and he gave me no answer. I said it once more, and the Prophet said to me: "Abu Hurayrah, whatever you shall have has been written and the ink has dried, and it will be the same whether you emasculate yourself or not."' (Related by al-Bukhari)

The Prophet's Companions did not impose restrictions on women so as to stop them from taking part in social life and meeting men. They had two reasons for this: the first is that they were wise enough not to even think of disrupting life's activity which requires a good measure of female participation. The second is that they steered away from injustice. They would never behave unfairly to women and burden them with the responsibility of relieving them of their own feelings of temptation.

Factor 4: Excessive jealousy

Protectiveness of one's honour is of two types: natural, healthy and balanced jealousy which helps to protect one's honour against being trifled with or assaulted. This is a proper feeling for every Muslim to have. The other type is disallowed jealousy, because there is nothing suspicious to arouse it. Thus, it is excessive and sickly. It tortures the jealous person and leads to false accusations. It might cause a person to lose focus and commit an assault on an innocent one. Moreover, such jealousy disrupts healthy life activity. The Prophet tells the truth as he says: 'Some jealousy is loved by God and some He hates. The one which God loves is that confined to real suspicion, while God dislikes jealousy when there is no reason for suspicion.' (Related by Abu Dāwūd)

It is true that some of the Prophet's Companions were particularly jealous. 'Umar ibn al-Khaṭṭāb and al-Zubayr ibn al-'Awwām were two such people. As regards 'Umar we have the following hadith:

Abu Hurayrah narrated: 'We were with the Prophet when he said: "As I was asleep, I saw myself in Heaven. I saw a woman performing the ablution close to a palace. I asked whose palace it was, and I was told that it belonged to 'Umar. I remembered how jealous he was and I turned back." 'Umar wept and said: "Would I be jealous of you, Messenger of God?"' (Related by al-Bukhari and Muslim)

Asmā' bint Abu Bakr, al-Zubayr's wife tells of his jealousy: 'I was coming back one day, carrying the date stones on my head. I met the Prophet on his camel with a group of the Anṣār. He called me, and started to make his camel sit. He wanted me to ride behind him. I felt too shy to be with all those men. I remembered that al-Zubayr was the most jealous of people. God's Messenger realized that I was too shy, and he went on.' (Related by al-Bukhari and Muslim)

By the grace of God, those Companions of the Prophet dealt with their jealousy by the implementation of Islamic rules, as we have seen in the case of 'Umar's wife: 'One of 'Umar's wives regularly attended the Fajr and 'Isha prayers with the congregation at the mosque. She was asked: "Why do you come out for these prayers when you know that 'Umar dislikes this and is jealous?" She said: "Why does he not stop me?" They said: "He is prevented by the Prophet's order: 'Do not stop women servants of God from attending God's mosques.'"' (Related by al-Bukhari)

When the best of generations, i.e. the generation of the Prophet's Companions, ended, jealousy began to go unchecked by its religious controls. It broke the barrier Islam sets up through the hadith: 'Do not prevent God's female servants from attending God's mosques.' Thus, Muslim women were stopped from going to the mosque, when the mosque was, particularly in the early generations, the main centre of worship, education as well as social and political activity.

ʿUmar ibn al-Khaṭṭāb restrained and controlled his jealousy, abiding by the Prophet's order not to stop women from attending the mosque. We note that his grandson, Bilāl ibn ʿAbdullāh ibn ʿUmar, did not control his jealousy, because it was fed by his unfounded suspicion. He declared: 'We shall stop them,' supporting his attitude by claiming that it is a case of 'cause prevention', saying: 'lest they use it as a cover for something untoward.' ʿAbdullāh ibn ʿUmar did not accept this argument from his son, emphasizing that he must abide by the Prophet's Sunnah.

Such excessive and unhealthy jealousy had to incline on some religious support and it found this in the claim for cause prevention. People supported such claims by arbitrarily giving a wrong interpretation of an authentic report. For example, they cite this statement by ʿĀ'ishah: 'Had the Prophet seen what women have perpetrated, he would have stopped them attending the mosque, as the Israelite women were stopped.' (Related by al-Bukhari and Muslim) They cite this statement as though it abrogates the Prophet's hadith: 'Do not stop God's female servants attending God's mosques.' Alternatively, they quote some hadiths which are poor in authenticity or even fabricated because they state that only elderly women used to attend the Prophet's mosques. We will say more about both these arguments presently.

Some eminent scholars express views that reflect such excessive jealousy, supporting it by fabricated reports or ones that lack authenticity. Yet, these reports are contrary to hadiths that are highly authentic, related by both al-Bukhari and Muslim. Here is an example of such statements:

> The proper way that stops jealousy is that men do not visit women and that women do not go out. The Prophet (peace be upon him) said to his daughter Fāṭimah: 'What is the best thing for a woman?' She said: 'That she sees no man

and that no man sees her.' He hugged her and said: '[such is) the offspring of one another.'[17] He liked her answer. The Prophet's Companions used to block holes and openings in the walls of their homes, so that women could not look at men. Muʿādh saw his wife looking through a slit in the wall and he hit her. He saw his wife giving a piece of an apple she was eating and he hit her. 'Umar said: 'Give women poor clothing and they will stay at home.' He said this because women do not like to go out with a poor outfit. He also said: 'Make it a habit to say "No" to your women.' God's Messenger (peace be upon him) had permitted women to attend the mosque, but the right way now is to stop them, except the elderly women.[18]

As years and centuries rolled on, and as some practices of the old ways that prevailed in the conquered areas crept into the Muslim society, as well as some remnants of the old Arabian ways of ignorance, protective jealousy became increasingly excessive. In some Muslim communities, a man would feel jealous if people saw his mother's or sister's or wife's face, or even if they heard her speaking without seeing her. This went even further, to the extent that a man would disdain to mention his wife's name, even for a very important reason. He considered mentioning her name as a slur on his honour.

It would have been well to state the true reason for this attitude and attribute it to personal preference by some men who are excessively jealous. However, people do not do this. Instead, they try to clothe this with a religious justification, which is definitely unfounded. They claim that it is all for protecting honour and preventing immorality!

17. This hadith is very poor in authenticity.
18. Al-Ghazālī, *Iḥyā' 'Ulūm al-Dīn*, Vol. 4, p. 142.

Factor 5: The claim of the spread of immorality

Some people always harp on the theme of times changing and the spread of immorality and indecency, as though people have become devoid of all goodness and that nothing could be worse than the present situation. They suggest that the Last Hour is very close and that it is better to be in the grave, rather than above ground. We, thus, have repeated warnings of impending doom. They cry over the 'good old days', when everything was fine, high morality prevailed and people were serious in their obedience of God and keen to do all that pleases Him. Such excessive claims tend to feed the feeling of despair among people, discouraging them from trying to improve things, and make them feel that trying to enjoin right and prevent evil is useless. In addition, such claims provide strong encouragement for the extremist application of the rule of cause prevention. As immorality is thought to spread, the need is greater to block its sources, even though these are permissible practices.

The extreme application of cause prevention is something that will never be satisfied; it will always ask for more. It will attack every aspect of mixing of the two sexes. When it has devoured all that is permissible, drawing a curtain of prevention over them all, it turns to what is recommended, then what is required as a duty and deals the same treatment to them all. Permissible practices that have been disallowed include men's greeting of women and women's greeting of men, women's attendance of congregational prayer in mosques and women's participation with men in paying visits, receiving guests and professional work. Recommended practices that have been disallowed include women's pursuit of religious education under male scholars, a man seeing the woman when he is proposing to marry her, all aspects of care a woman may offer to her male relatives, such as visiting them when they are ill, offering condolences in cases of bereavement, etc. Duties that have also been stopped include women's returning men's greetings, attending the Eid Prayer as well as enjoining what is right and censuring what is evil.

It is also part of the nature of extremism that it continues to acquire strength and becomes well rooted as the years roll on. It always cites the argument that times have changed and corruption has spread. Here are some examples:

Conversation between men and women: It was the practice during the Prophet's lifetime that men and women talked to each other, without a screen between them. Only the Prophet's wives were screened when this was commanded by God. This is explained in detail in Chapter 4 of Volume 2 of this series. With time, all women were prevented from talking to men except from behind a screen, because of the claim that times had changed and immorality had spread. Therefore, all women are more in need to be screened than the Prophet's wives who were the purest of women. We devoted Chapter 2 of Volume 5 of this series to show that screening applied only to the Prophet's wives and that the argument that other women should do the same is false. Yet the matter did not stop at that, as women were also stopped from talking to men, even from behind a screen, because of the claim that 'a woman's voice is part of her *'awrah*' and causes temptation, particularly because men's moral standards had weakened due to the changing times.

Women's attending prayer in the mosque: It was the Prophet's constant practice that a number of women, young, adult and elderly frequented the mosque to join the congregational prayer. This is explained in Chapter 4 of Volume 2 in this series. Yet it was not long after the Prophet had passed away that the tendency became one of stopping women going to the mosque. Bilāl ibn 'Abdullāh ibn 'Umar declared that this was needed so that going to the mosque would not be used as a cover for something untoward. Imam al-Ghazālī comments that Bilāl 'dared to express disagreement because of his knowledge that times had changed.'[19] As time passed, young

19. Al-Ghazālī, ibid, p. 142.

and adult women were stopped from attending mosques. A woman's husband or guardian was recommended not to allow her to go to the mosque, because times had changed. Elderly women, however, continued to be allowed to go to the mosque. Yet even they were subsequently stopped from going to the mosque, because when a woman prays, she uncovers her face and men could see her. As times have changed, it is argued that even elderly women present temptation!

Attending the Eid prayer: The Prophet's practice was that all women, including young girls who have just attained puberty, and menstruating women, should attend the Eid Prayer, to take part both in the prayer and the celebration of Eid Day. This is discussed in detail in Chapter 4 in Volume 2 of this series. However, as time went on, young women were stopped from attending the Eid Prayer. Ḥafṣah bint Sīrīn, who belonged to the *tābi'īn* generation which immediately followed the Prophet's Companions' generation, said: 'We used to prevent our young women coming out on the two Eids.' (Related by al-Bukhari) Imam Ibn Ḥajar comments: 'It appears as though they stopped young women coming out because of the increase in immorality taking place after the first generation.' As centuries passed, adult women were also prevented, allowing only elderly women to attend the Eid Prayer. Then as time rolled by, even elderly women were stopped because they were also thought to incite temptation!

Some people frequently speak about times changing, allowing immorality to spread. They use this as an argument for stricter implementation of the rule of cause prevention. However, they overlook the fact that such frequent reference to the spread of immorality discourages people from trying to introduce reform. What is needed is a moderate assessment of the good and the evil in people's lives, so as to formulate an accurate concept of their situation. The fact is that although the situation of a particular community may reflect much that is bad, it also contains good things, and these are the keys to strengthen hope and to initiate reform. In order for reform to be successful, some good people must be available and the community generally must have some good aspects. With these together, a community may reform itself and proceed on the way to progress. They will be able to set a plan of reform to stamp out deviant practices, leaving no room for despair and surrender to the spreading evil.

What confirms the presence of goodness in all times is that every generation extols the praises of the goodness that prevailed in the time of their parents and grandparents while lamenting the spread of evil and corruption in their own time. A hadith related by al-Bukhari mentions that the signs of the Last Hour include that 'time will shrink, knowledge will decrease, stinginess will be manifest, trials will spread and killing will increase.' In his *Fatḥ al-Bārī*, a voluminous commentary on al-Bukhari's *Ṣaḥīḥ*, Imam Ibn Ḥajar quotes Ibn Baṭṭāl: 'We have seen with our own eyes all these signs mentioned in this hadith: knowledge has decreased, ignorance has become clearly apparent, stinginess is seen to take root in people's hearts, trials are widespread and killing has increased.' Ibn Ḥajar comments on this statement: 'It appears that what Ibn Baṭṭāl had seen was in plenty, but these were present together with their opposites of good things. What the hadith refers to is that these evils will become predominant when only little of what is good exists in opposition... The fact is that the beginnings of these situations started in the time of the Prophet's Companions. They then increased in some places, but not in others. The situation that augurs the occurrence of the Last Hour is that they will become predominant, as I have said.'

A number of highly respectable people spoke about how things were during the Prophet's lifetime. (1) The following is attributed to Anas ibn Mālik: 'I do not recognize anything as it used to be during the Prophet's lifetime.' Some people said: 'How about prayer?' He said: 'Have you not done it your own way?' He was referring to delaying offering prayers. (2) Mālik ibn Abi Sahl ibn Mālik quotes his father who was one of the distinguished *tābiʿīn*. He said: 'The only thing I recognize of what people used to be (meaning the Prophet's Companions) is the call to prayer.' Both these statements highlight the merits of the first generation and their high standards. They also imply a warning against deviating from the Prophet's Sunnah and the practice of his noble Companions. (3) Mālik was asked about the people of Madinah and Makkah letting their slave women go out with parts of their chests and shoulders uncovered, and that slave women were exhibited for sale with only the bottom half of their bodies covered. He expressed strong disapproval and said: 'This was not the practice of the good and knowledgeable people of the past, and it is not what is allowed by scholars and good people. It is the practice of people who are devoid of piety.' (4) Hishām ibn 'Urwah ibn al-Zubayr said: 'When 'Urwah moved to his palace at al-'Aqīq, people took issue with him and said to him: "You have deserted the Prophet's mosque." He said: "I have noted that there is much distraction in your mosques, and much idle talk in your marketplace. There is plenty of apparent indecency in your streets. Therefore, I felt that I better remove myself from what you indulge in."' People said: 'If 'Urwah mentions this of Madinah, how can its people's practice be cited as evidence, when it is not confirmed by a text?' Abu 'Umar said: 'My view is that in *al-Muwaṭṭa'* and other situations, Mālik refers to the practice of the scholars and pious people of Madinah, not that of the ignorant public.' These two statements make clear that in every age there are people of knowledge and goodness as well as others who are ignorant and devoid of piety. The latter will commit what is deviant from the Prophet's guidance.

The argument of changed times is complemented by the claim that the rulings of the Shariah, which are mild and easy, were given at the time of those who were at a very high standard of purity and piety. As times have changed, these rulings are no longer suitable. Therefore, the only way to prevent corruption is to impose restrictions, changing the easy rulings that prevailed during the Prophet's lifetime and his rightly-guided successors, related to women's participation in social life and meeting men, even though this meeting is in a mosque and during prayer. One example of the argument that the fine age of purity and piety has gone is the statement: 'That Abu Bakr and Anas met Umm Ayman does not necessarily mean that they looked at her. Besides, these people cannot be taken as a model for others. They could meet a woman privately.'[20]

In response to this extreme attitude of restriction, we cite what Imam al-Ḥaramayn al-Juwaynī says about those who do not abide by the easy rules God has established:

> They claim that what took place in the early period of Islam and all the easy rulings given were because they were close to the purest form of Islam. It was enough to give a gentle reminder or little admonition for them to be deterred. Now that hearts are hardened, times have gone by and pledges are weak, most people cling to their desires and their fears. Were we to limit punishment to what it was like, that would be unwise.
>
> This sort of discourse may appeal to the ignorant, but in truth it leads to the contrary of the message of the greatest Prophet. In short, whoever thinks that the Shariah may be derived from what wise and logical people think actually rejects the Shariah. What he says will be taken as a means to rejecting the divine message...
>
> Such argument is nothing but wayward thinking. Were they to be imposed on religious rules, everyone who has a shred of logic will treat his own thinking as a law that commands and prohibits. Thus, people's inclinations and preferences

20. Al-Anṣārī, *Nihāyat al-Muḥtāj ilā Sharḥ al-Minhāj*, Vol. 6, p. 188.

> will replace God's revelations to His messengers. Moreover, such dictates will change with time and place, and there will no longer be any firm place for the divine law...
>
> The truth to be followed is what reliable scholars have narrated from the Prophet, the noblest of mankind. Nothing that differs with it is admissible. What is left, apart from the truth, except error?
>
> A person who steers away from the controls established by the religion is one who does not appreciate its beauty, nor understands its aims and purposes. Were such a person to look hard at any good value, he will certainly find it, or find something better, in God's law... This is the proper way and the right direction. Whatever else is excess and going beyond the limits. It is moving towards the extreme. Prophets were sent to state clear rules and wise measures.[21]

Another element that strengthened the claim of the spread of corruption and led to greater strictness in the application of the rule of cause prevention is preferring the safer course. One example is the claim: 'It is forbidden to look at the *'awrah* of an adult woman, which is all her body apart from her face and hands. This is based on the Qur'anic verse that says: "Tell believing men to lower their gaze." It also applies to her face and hands when temptation is feared... It also applies when a person thinks himself safe from temptation, according to the correct view. This is explained by the fact that looking is assumed to cause temptation and incite desire. What is appropriate of the Shariah is to close the means and ignore the details of different situations, such as seclusion with a woman who is a stranger. Thus, the argument that "since it is not *'awrah*, how come looking at it is forbidden?" The answer is that although it is

21. Imam al-Ḥaramayn, *al-Ghiyāthī*, Vol. 2, p. 138.

not *'awrah*, looking at it is thought to cause temptation or stir desire. Therefore, it is safer to wean people away from it.'[22]

An eminent contemporary scholar rightly rejects the preference of the 'safer option': 'My long study and practice make it clear to me that direct reference to the Qur'an and the Sunnah always brings about an easy and gentle way, moving away from causing difficulty and hardship. This is the opposite of referring to the rules of schools of Fiqh which have been burdened over the centuries with numerous additional restrictions, resorting to preferring what is thought to be safer. When religion becomes a long list of safer options, it loses its spirit of ease, replacing it with hardship, while God kept it free of hardship as He says: "He has laid no hardship on you in religion."[23] (22: 78)

Several centuries ago, leading scholars rejected the need to take the safer option. Imam al-Ḥaramayn said: 'If it is said: Should we not take the safer option? We answer that there is no rule in Islam stating that when something is doubtful to be a duty it must be upheld as a duty.' Ibn Taymiyyah said: 'The principles of the Shariah confirm that choosing what is safer is neither obligatory nor forbidden.'

We certainly appreciate the position of those who take a view contrary to ours. They are grieved by what they see of immorality, but like their predecessors, they exaggerate the extent of immorality to the point that they overlook the benefits of women's participation in social life and meeting with men, and the hardship caused by preventing these.

Factor 6: A number of Qur'anic verses, hadiths and reports

We have already discussed some factors leading to extremism in the application of the rule of cause prevention. What is amazing

22. Al-Anṣārī, op cit., pp. 187-8.
23. Yusuf al-Qaradawi, *Fatāwā Mu'āṣirah*, Vol. 1, p. 6.

is that these factors have found support in a number of texts and statements, including some Qur'anic verses and hadiths that are wrongly interpreted, and other hadiths that either lack authenticity or are outrightly fabricated. In addition, there are some flimsy reports. We will give some examples of all these.

One: Verses, hadiths and reports confirming mistrust of women

1. Qur'anic verses wrongly interpreted: 'Your (i.e. women's) guile is awesome indeed.' (12: 28). This statement is not one that God has said about women generally. It was the word of the nobleman in whose home Joseph was brought up. He said it in comment on what his wife had done. The fact that the Qur'an quotes his words does not mean an endorsement of what he said and that it is God's view of the nature of all women across all generations.

   We should reflect on the guile of Joseph's brothers and how they schemed against him. They resorted to an elaborate trick, with foul preliminaries, an evil deed, followed by blatant lies and wicked forgery. God says: 'They said (to their father): "Father, Why do you not trust us with Joseph, when we are indeed his well-wishers? Send him with us tomorrow, that he may enjoy himself and play. We will certainly take good care of him." He answered: "It certainly grieves me that you should take him with you; and I dread that the wolf may eat him when you are heedless of him." They said: 'If the wolf were to eat him when we are so many, then we should surely be lost.' And when they went away with him, they resolved to cast him into the depth of the well. We revealed [this] to him: You will tell them of this their deed at a time when they shall not know you. At nightfall they came to their father weeping, and said: 'Father, we went off racing and left Joseph behind with our belongings, and the wolf devoured him. But you will not believe us even though we are saying the truth.' And they produced his shirt stained with false blood. He said: "No, but your minds have tempted you to evil. Sweet patience! It is to God alone that I turn for support in this misfortune that you have described.'" (12: 11-18). Should we ask: which guile is greater in this case: men's or women's?

2. Authentic hadiths that have been wrongly interpreted:

   - Women are 'deficient in mind and religion.' This hadith is given such wrong interpretation that people came to think that women are no better than morons. The Prophet, however, explained that the deficiency is in her mental activity and ability to act as a witness in matters of business. This is an area that is largely unfamiliar to women who are mostly housewives. The Prophet accepted the testimony of only one woman in cases of breastfeeding.[24] Scholars also have approved the testimony of two women in feminine matters.
   - 'A woman is created from a rib, and the most crooked part of a rib is its top part....' This hadith is so misinterpreted that some people said that women have a deceitful nature. The fact is that the hadith refers to a distinctive aspect of the creation of women, which affects her behaviour in a way that a man may find irritating. Crooked is the opposite of 'straight', and a woman's crookedness refers to her quick and strong reaction, while a balanced and controlled reaction reflects being straight. The Creator, in His infinite wisdom, has given the woman this strong reaction so that she is emotionally caring and tender, which is very necessary for the upbringing of her children. We discussed these two hadiths in detail in Chapter 6 of Volume 1 of this series.

24. It is sufficient that one woman testifies that she had breastfed a man, when he was a suckling child, for that man to be considered as her son, blocking his marriage to any female of her own family. On the other hand, in matters that are peculiar to women, men's testimonies are disregarded, while two women are accepted as witnesses.

- 'If any bad omen is true, it applies to the woman, horse and house.' This hadith is wrongly interpreted because of mistakes that occurred in some of its versions, because of an abridgement in its text, or error by some narrators. It is often quoted by people as: 'A bad omen is in three things', or 'A bad omen is only in three things.' As a result, women became one of the sources of bad omens. Islam denounces bad omens generally and approves of good omens. God's Messenger says: 'There is no bad omen, but a good omen may be in a home, a woman and in a horse.'

3. Hadiths lacking authenticity:

   - 'A pious woman is as rare among women as a crow with one white leg.'
   - 'Women are like toys. Whoever wants to have a toy should choose a good one.'

By contrast, an authentic hadith quotes the Prophet: 'Women are men's full sisters.'

- 'Men were ruined when they obeyed women.'

Abu Bakr ibn al-ʿArabī totally disapproves of the circulation of hadiths that are poor in authenticity. He says: 'People must be as careful in respect of their faith as they are in respect of their money. No one who sells something would accept defective currency for it. They will only choose what is proper and legal tender. Likewise, the only narrations from the Prophet that may be upheld are those that are narrated with sound and authentic chains of transmission. Otherwise, they may find themselves floundering in an area that attributes a falsehood to the Prophet. While they look for hadiths to learn what is useful, they end up with what is useless, or may indeed find themselves in total loss.'[25]

4. False, fabricated hadiths:

   - 'I have been favoured above Adam by two qualities: the first is that his wife helped him to disobey God, while my wives help me to obey Him....'
   - 'Obeying women lands one in sorrow.'
   - 'Consult women but do not take their advice.'

Yet an authentic hadith confirms that God's Messenger (peace be upon him) acted on his wife's, Umm Salamah's, advice at the time of al-Ḥudaybiyah, and that her advice was a blessing.

   - 'Were it not for women, God would have been truly and properly worshipped.'
   - 'Were it not for women, men would have been in Heaven.'
   - 'Do not teach women writing, and do not house them in homes. Teach them Surah 24, Light.'

Yet an authentic hadith narrated by al-Shifā' bint 'Abdullāh says: 'The Prophet (peace be upon him) came in when I was visiting Ḥafṣah. He said to me: 'Teach her (i.e. Ḥafṣah) the supplication for the cure of *namlah* (which is skin inflammation on one's side) as you taught her to write.'

   - 'Burying girls is a blessing.'

The false hadith that says, 'Do not teach women writing', was the pinnacle of extremism. It prevailed in people's thinking until the early twentieth century in most countries of the Muslim

25. Quoted by al-Qurṭubī in his commentary on the Qur'an, Vol. 14, p. 235.

world. By the grace of God, it began to be discarded, as some good scholars showed it to be false. Nevertheless, it continued to be cited in some countries until the mid-twentieth century. Dr Taqiy al-Dīn al-Hilālī explains this type of extremism:

> There are three different views about the education and upbringing of girls. The first advocates limiting their education to reading the Qur'an without understanding it. Those who hold this view say that this is the best and most correct view. It is the practice of our fathers, and they were better people than us. Educating women will corrupt their morality. A woman who neither reads nor writes remains safe from human devils. As everyone knows, the pen is one of the two tongues a person has. When a woman does not learn reading and writing, she is safe from the evil of this tongue, and when she is strictly covered, the other tongue is rendered safe, and she is thus safe from evil. We have seen many women who landed into evil only because of their education. This took place in the good time of Islamic values, good manners and Arabian high regard of honour. By contrast, our age suffers great deterioration in these standards, rendering reform a distant goal. When a girl learns reading, she has access to every type of immorality that occurs in this world. Her mind becomes full of evil thoughts that she used to be spared. A hadith advises us: 'Do not house women in homes, and do not teach them writing. Teach them sewing and Surah 24, Light.' This is the good education, while teaching women writing facilitates for them writing to transgressors, and housing them in homes facilitates for them contact with wicked people, even by signals.[26]

26. T. al-Hilālī, *Ta'līm al-Ināth wa Tarbiyatahunn*, a booklet published by al-Tamaddun al-Islamī, Damascus, 1953.

Imam Ibn Ḥajar shows the fallacy of the argument that justifies fabricating hadiths for an alleged religious interest. He says: 'The Karrāmiyyah and a few others suggest that it is permissible to lie for the Prophet in order to further the cause of religion and to support the way of following the Sunnah, as well as to encourage compliance and warn against disobedience. They argue that the Prophet's warning refers to attributing a false statement to him which is against his guidance, but not for making such a false statement to support him. This is a false argument. The warning applies to whoever attributes to the Prophet anything false, whether for or against his message. The faith is perfect, by God's grace, and it does not need lies to strengthen its cause.'[27]

One example of such lies is that someone noticed that people felt gloomy when a daughter was born to them. He wanted them to stop this wrongful attitude and he fabricated a hadith saying: 'One of the woman's blessings is that her first child is a girl.'

5. Unauthentic and fabricated reports:

    - It is reported that Luqmān passed by a young girl learning in the local school. He said: 'For whom has this sword been sharpened?' meaning sharpened to kill.
    - It is reported that 'Umar ibn al-Khaṭṭāb said: 'Contradict women, for contradicting them brings a blessing.'
    - It is reported that a woman from 'Umar ibn 'Abd al-'Azīz's household died. When she was buried and he returned with other people, they wanted to offer their condolences to him when he reached his home. However, he went in and closed the door. He said: 'We do not accept condolences for the loss of women.'

27. Ibn Ḥajar, *Fatḥ al-Bārī*, Vol. 7, p. 310.

Muhammad ibn Muhammad, the author of *Mawāhib al-Jalīl fi Sharḥ Mukhtaṣar Khalīl*, refutes this report. He says: 'The Prophet said: "Whoever loses three of his children and accepts their loss with resignation shall be admitted to Heaven." He did not distinguish boys from girls. God says: "The calamity of death may be befalling you." (5: 106) The Prophet said: "Let Muslims console themselves when they suffer a calamity by citing the calamity of my loss. He considered the loss of a good wife and a good friend to be a calamity."'

Two: Verses, hadiths and reports confirming the misunderstanding of the meaning of female temptation

1. Misunderstood verses:

   - God says: 'When you ask them for something, do so from behind a screen: this makes for greater purity for your hearts and theirs.' (33: 53)

The verse states that staying behind a screen was obligatory for the Prophet's wives in particular. Some people misunderstand the verse and make this obligatory or recommended for all Muslim women. We have proven that this screening applied only to the Prophet's wives and there is no suggestion that other Muslim women should do the same. This is clearly stated in Chapter 2 of Volume 5 of this series.

   - 'Stay quietly in your homes, and do not display your charms as women used to display them in the old days of pagan ignorance.' (33:33) The misunderstanding of this verse is discussed in detail in Chapter 1 of Volume 5 of this series.

2. Authentic hadiths given erroneous interpretation:

We will only mention here two such hadiths, pointing out that the correct meaning of these two hadiths as well as many more authentic and misunderstood hadiths are discussed at length in Chapter 1 of Volume 5 of this series. Such misinterpretation has contributed to the extremism in the application of cause prevention.

- The hadith narrated by Umm Salamah: 'I was at God's Messenger's (peace be upon him) and Maymūnah was with him when Ibn Umm Maktūm came over. This was after we were commanded to be screened. The Prophet said to us: "Go behind a screen." We said: "Messenger of God, is he not blind and cannot see or recognize us?" The Prophet said: "Are you two also blind? Do you not see him?"'

Some people understood the hadith as applicable to all Muslim women, when it is only applicable to the Prophet's wives.

- The Prophet said: 'Beware of entry of women's places.' A man from the Anṣār said: 'Messenger of God, how about an in-law relative?' He said: 'An in-law is death.'

People interpreted the hadith as a prohibition of entering women's places at all times, while it means that people must not enter their places when a woman is alone.

In addition, some authentic reports have been wrongly understood. One such example is 'Ā'ishah's statement: 'Had the Prophet seen what women have perpetrated, he would have stopped them attending the mosque, as the Israelite women were stopped.' People interpreted her statement as a requirement that stopped women from going to mosques, as if it abrogates what the Prophet says: 'Do not stop women servants of God from attending God's mosques.' However, 'Ā'ishah's statement refers to women who did the opposite of the Prophet's teachings whereby women should not wear adornments or perfume when they go to mosques.

3. Hadiths lacking authenticity:

   - Men may greet women, but women may not greet men.
   - Strengthen yourselves against women by keeping them in poor clothing.
   - Keep women poorly clothed and they will stay at home.
   - Bury women's shame in homes.
   - The Prophet prohibited women from going out, except an elderly woman wearing worn-out shoes.
   - The Prophet (peace be upon him) said to his daughter Fāṭimah: 'What is the best thing for a woman?' She said: 'That she sees no man and that no man sees her.' He hugged her and said: '(such is) the offspring of one another.'
   - Umm Salamah bint Ḥakīm said: 'I saw elderly women praying obligatory prayers with God's Messenger (peace be upon him).'
   - Sulaymān ibn Abi Ḥathamah narrated from his mother, that she said: 'I saw elderly women praying with God's Messenger (peace be upon him) in the mosque.'
   - The work of any of you in her home earns her the reward of jihad by fighters for God's cause, God willing.

We cited in Chapter 4 of Volume 2 of this series many authentic hadiths urging young women to attend the congregational prayers with God's Messenger (peace be upon him). These women included Asmā' bint Abu Bakr, 'Ātikah bint Zayd who was 'Umar ibn al-Khaṭṭāb's wife, Fāṭimah bint Qays and al-Rubayyiʿ bint Muʿawwidh.

4. False and fabricated hadiths:

   - A woman has two covers: the grave and her husband.
   - God's Messenger (peace be upon him) prohibited a man from walking between two women.
   - The delegation from the ʿAbd al-Qays tribe came over, and they included a lad who was exceptionally handsome. The Prophet (peace be upon him) sat him behind his back and said: 'Prophet David's sin was looking.'

Those who hold the strict view say that if this is the Prophet's guidance in respect of the temptation arising from a handsome lad, such temptation is greater and more serious in the case of women. Therefore, keeping women away from men is more preferable.

5. Unauthentic reports:

   - It is discouraged that men greet women or women greet men.
   - It is claimed that ʿAbdullāh ibn Masʿūd said: 'No woman offers a prayer better than her prayer at home, except for the two mosques in Makkah and Madinah, except an old woman wearing worn-out shoes.'

Conclusion

When we look carefully at the factors that helped and added to the excessive application of the rule of cause prevention, we find that there was always the element of following conjecture or following prejudice, or both. Conjecture is the opposite of confirmed knowledge. Knowledge means understanding the reality of things and awareness of rulings along with the evidence supporting such rulings. Conjecture relies on deceptive matters, such as unauthentic reports, deficient information or misconceptions. On the other hand, prejudice blinds a person to the truth which God has revealed, even though its light makes it very clear. Indeed, prejudice leaves a person blindfolded, turning around oneself, unable to see anything clearly.

The claim of protecting one's honour is the result of following conjecture which confuses people's weak adherence to their faith with the increase of immoral behaviour as a result of doing what is permissible. It is also caused by relying on deficient and unreliable information in one's assessment of realities. Prejudice is another contributing factor, as it leads to confusing proper jealousy with the excessive type.

The urge to choose the safer option is also motivated by following conjecture. Its advocates imagine that taking the safer option in preference to what is permissible is a mark of real piety. Moreover, it is sometimes motivated by following prejudice. In fact, prejudice is not confined to just an inclination towards what is forbidden. Some people lean towards making things even harder for themselves and others, urging them to forgo what is permissible.

The circulation of hadiths that are either poor in authenticity or outright fabrication is also based on following conjecture. People wrongly imagine that such hadiths are more effective in urging people to keep on the right track, obeying God, and steering away from sin. It may also have an element of following prejudice.

A common element to all these factors that leads to the excessive application of cause prevention is that of following conjecture, which relies on social tradition. This is what we may call 'compounded unawareness.' Sticking to tradition leads to unawareness of the relevant religious texts. A quick glance at Volume 2 is sufficient to clearly show that there is general unawareness of the texts of the Sunnah which confirm that women's participation in social life and their meeting with men in an atmosphere of seriousness and propriety were part of the Prophet's guidance and features of Islamic society. Moreover, sticking to tradition leads to unawareness and misunderstanding of Fiqh principles. We quoted at length from what scholars of legal theory wrote about the implementation of cause prevention. They definitely show that two essential conditions for the implementation of this rule are largely ignored or overlooked. The first of these conditions is that the permissible practice that is prevented under this rule should lead to harm or a negative result in most cases. The second condition is that its negative result should be greater than its benefit.

Had the matter been confined to following conjecture, the problem would have been easier, because increased knowledge of the Qur'an, the Sunnah, the principles of Fiqh and legal theory, as well as knowledge of social phenomena would be enough to overcome it. By contrast, dealing with the question of following prejudice is far more difficult, because prejudice seals minds and hearts. We hope that we have been successful, to some extent, in providing the necessary information as also exposing hardened prejudice. We should all remember the following verses: 'They [who disbelieve) follow nothing but conjecture and the whims of their own souls, even though right guidance from their Lord has now come to them.' (53: 23) 'They follow nothing but conjecture, but conjecture can never take the place of truth.' (53: 28)

Finally, we say that the temptation that is occasioned by uncovering women's faces and their participation in legitimate social life is part of the trial to which God subjects men and women in their daily activities. That Muslims endure this trial and resist the temptation will strengthen their will and enhance their resistance to their desire. The ultimate outcome is that a Muslim will have an upright and healthy personality. To try to evade this temptation only means the imposition of arbitrary restrictions, which can never lead to good results. We mentioned earlier that Abu Hurayrah wanted to evade this temptation. The Prophet stated his categorical disapproval and said to him: 'Abu Hurayrah, whatever you shall have has been written and the ink has dried, and it will be the same whether you emasculate yourself or not.'

Cause prevention is a rule of Islamic law, but its implementation cannot be described as complying with Islamic law unless it fulfils the conditions outlined by the scholars of legal theory. To ignore these conditions leads to the sin of abandoning Islamic law.

The Prophet's companions and leading scholars who followed their example applied this rule to prevent the causes of confusing the rulings of Islamic law. In this context, we quoted what al-Shāṭibī said concerning the duty of explaining what is permissible. It is most strange that later generations should apply the same rule to confuse the rulings of Islamic law. In other words, their strict extremism in the application of this rule led to confusing many permissible matters with what is discouraged or prohibited. We pray to God to guide us all to the truth.